WILLIAM MORRIS
by himself

WILLIAM MORRIS
by himself

Designs and writings

Edited by Gillian Naylor

LITTLE, BROWN AND COMPANY

BOSTON   NEW YORK   LONDON

TITLE PAGE: WOMAN PLAYING CYMBALS, *c*.1875

A LITTLE, BROWN Book

First published in Great Britain in 1988
by Macdonald & Co (Publishers)
Reprinted 1990 by Macdonald & Co (Publishers)
Reprinted 1994 and 1996 (paperback)
by Little, Brown and Company

This edition published in 2000 by Little, Brown and Company (UK)

A CIP catalogue record for this book is available
from the British Library

ISBN 0-316-85507-3

Editors: Sarah Chapman, Elizabeth Eyres
Text Editor: Mary Trewby
Design: Adrian Morris
Picture Research: Helena Beaufoy, Jessica Walton
Art Director: Linda Cole
Production by Omnipress
Printed in Spain

Little, Brown and Company (UK)
Brettenham House
Lancaster Place
London WC2E 7EN

For Denny

Acknowledgements

The Society of Antiquaries, Trustees of the William Morris Estate,
gave overall permission for the publication of the material presented
in this book, and for the photography at Kelmscott Manor. Apart
from unpublished material studied in British Collections (The
National Art Library, The William Morris Gallery, and the British
Museum), the Princeton University Press kindly gave permission for
the use of letters published in *The Collected Letters of William
Morris*, Vol. I, edited by Norman Kelvin. Permission to reproduce
extracts from E.P. Thompson's *William Morris: Romantic to
Revolutionary* was kindly given by the Merlin Press.
  The editorial staff of Macdonald Orbis have been supportive and
efficient throughout, and I would also like to thank Mary Trewby
for her positive as well as painstaking help with the editing.
  The picture research and co-ordination of the photography was
under the direction of Helena Beaufoy, who was responsible for the
range as well as the quality of the illustrations, which, of course, is
what *William Morris by himself* is all about.
  My colleagues in the Library at the Royal College of Art were, as
ever, patient, cheerful and helpful.

                                                        Gillian Naylor

The publishers would like to thank Helen Sloan and Nora Gillow of the
William Morris Gallery for their generous help with organizing
photography and answering numerous queries, and also The National
Trust, Sandford Berger and The Society of Antiquaries for their
permission to photograph from their collections.
  Flower arrangements by Pot Pourri, Chiswick, London

Editor's Note

Since William Morris wrote so much throughout his life (May
Morris's *Collected Works* runs to 24 volumes, and there is also
unpublished material), it has only been possible to present a
selection of his writing in this book. This selection, obviously, was
very difficult to make, and there are regrettable omissions, most
notably coverage of William Morris's re-telling, or his translations,
of the Nordic Sagas. Morris published his translation of the
Volsunga Saga in 1870, and his own *Sigurd the Volsung* in 1876. He
also published a translation of *The Odyssey* in 1887. Weighing up
the problems of content *v*. space, I decided to include a section from
Morris's first Icelandic journal (rather than extracts from the Saga
material), since the accounts are so vivid, and so rarely referred to
in other anthologies. I also decided to devote a whole section to the
correspondence with Thomas Wardle, because these letters relate so
directly to Morris's work, as well as to many of the illustrations.
  The material is presented in a broadly chronological framework;
in the interests of clarity and thematic accessibility, however, some
sections relate to specific subjects, so that, for example, there is a
section on Kelmscott Manor, and these sections include material
from a wide chronological time-span.
  Morris was not good at spelling ('dissappointing' was always a
pitfall for him); I have attempted to use his own spelling
throughout, although any enthousiasms [sic] are the editor's own.

CONTENTS

CARTOON FOR THE ANNUNCIATION, 1862

INTRODUCTION

'O how I long to keep the world from narrowing in on me, and to look at things bigly and kindly!'

In this book William Morris speaks for himself, and with a consistency that owes nothing to editorial selection. His message is clear and positive, but it is neither comfortable nor comforting; in spite of the lyricism and the brilliance of his designs, and in spite of his obvious zest for life, Morris speaks the language of alienation and confrontation. He was a man at odds with his own times, his own class and his own conscience, and he was determined to do something about it. This alienation, however, was not that of the misunderstood artist, destined, at best, to posthumous fame – Morris's achievements as a poet and a designer were acknowledged in his own lifetime, and his political radicalism did little to diminish his public stature. His achievements also did little to change the world, and therein lay his frustration: the fact that his poetry made suitable and soothing family reading, and that his wallpapers and fabrics embellished upper-middle-class homes in England and America, was of little comfort to him when so few were able to enjoy, or even recognize, the privileges that had contributed to the creation of this art. 'What business have we with art at all unless all can share it?' he asked in one of his first lectures. 'No man can exist in society and be neutral,' he stated in one of his last.

When he was a student at Oxford, writing poetry and romances for the magazine he was financing, and deciding to become an architect rather than a priest, Morris had described his work as 'the embodiment of dreams in one form or another'; he acknowledged 'that things are in a muddle', but felt he had 'no power or vocation to set them right'. He confirmed this conviction ten years later when he was writing *The Earthly Paradise*, and declaring himself an 'idle singer of an empty day'. In these early years, however, although the poetry and stories he wrote might have appeared to be a form of escapism, Morris was laying the foundations for his future commitment. As a child he is reputed to have read all Sir Walter Scott's *Waverley* novels before he was seven; he enacted scenes of chivalry (in a small suit of armour especially made for him) in the grounds of Woodford Hall, the substantial mansion in Epping Forest in which the family then lived, and at the same time he was learning to look, to remember, and, significantly, to interpret what he saw. At school at Marlborough he writes to his sister about an expedition to 'Abury' to see the mysterious stones there. He had been twice, because he needed to understand 'how they had been fixed', and while he was there he also visited the nearby church with 'four little spires on it of the decorated order', and a 'beautiful Norman doorway loaded with mouldings'. Morris was just fifteen, and even then his perception of landscape, and of buildings within a landscape, was remarkable; he needed to see, to categorize, to date, and above all to know *how* things had been done. Later he was to ask *why* things are the way they are, and it was his response to these questions that led him to social and political commitment.

In these early years William Morris's preoccupation with the past, like that of so many of his contemporaries, was both romantic and didactic. Nineteenth-century painters (his friend Burne-Jones, for example, who he met at Oxford, and the Pre-Raphaelites, who he was soon to meet), as well as writers, looked to the past for an old order of chivalry, self-confident in its hierarchies of honour and adventure; they looked for traditional and symbolic ideals of workmanship, and for a simple religious order dedicated to the welfare of both rich and poor. The past, to writers such as Thomas Carlyle (*Past and Present*, 1843), to proselytizers such as the architect Pugin (*Contrasts*, 1836), and to poets such as William Blake, was a mirror in which the poverty, the inhumanity and the infirmity of the present were reflected. Such writers lamented the destruction of an old social and religious order, and challenged the concepts of 'progress' associated with industrialization. Their concerns were to a certain extent nostalgic – the familiar laments of the radical conservative. They were complemented, however, by a growing demand for historical scholarship: studies of the nature and processes of history, which were reinforced by archaeological and anthropological research and attempts to dissect and categorize the buildings and the social order of the past. And at the same time, of course, imperialism was extending the boundaries as well as the implications of commerce: the 'Great Exhibition' of 1851, for example, was a display of the 'works of industry of all nations', so that there were now lessons to be learned from a world, rather than a national or European, culture.

As the son of a self-made man, William Morris, born in 1836, was a product of England's new social order. His father had made a small but judicious investment in a Devonshire copper mine (The Devon Great Consols), and had become extremely wealthy, securing for his family the comfort and the confidence of an upper-middle-class life-style. The young William seems to have enjoyed an idyllic childhood. He had his books, his pony, his personal suit of armour, a forest to play in and, apart from boredom on Sundays and some difficulty with spelling, nothing appears to have troubled him. He was homesick when he was at boarding school, but he had plenty of interests there, and the time to pursue them. He could read the books in the library (which was 'well-provided with works on archaeology and ecclesiastical architecture'), and began to 'read' the architecture of the locality – an interest introduced to him by his father. He also made up stories, 'vaguely described as "about knights and fairies", in which one adventure rose out of another, and the tale flowed on from day to day over a whole

term', according to his first biographer, J.W. Mackail.

He continued to make up stories when he went to Oxford, disquieting stories about death, obsession and isolation. 'I am the man that knows,' he wrote in 'Frank's Sealed Letter', 'that feels all poetry and art', and there is indeed a shamanistic quality about these romances, in which dream and reality, past and present, are fused and confused. In some of them the accounts of blows, battle and bloodshed recall the school-boy entertainment; in others – 'The Story of the Unknown Church', for example, and 'The Lindenborg Pool' – dreams (and nightmares) and presentiments of death weave a complex web of time past and time to come – the lifeless Lindenborg pool, and the remains of the unknown church surviving, in the narrative, to bear witness to the reality of the past. The extracts from the *Early Romances* published in this book convey something of these qualities; they have been chosen, however, to demonstrate Morris's powers of description, and for their evocations, based on his personal observations at the time, of landscapes, buildings, and craftsmanship.

Morris's poetry of this period speaks for itself. He wrote verse easily, fluently, and seemingly naïvely. This naïveté, however, is deceptive, for it gives his verse an immediacy that relates it to the present rather than the past. These are not ancient tales of betrayal and heroism that Morris is re-telling; for him they belong to the here and now. We are with Sir Peter Harpdon and his surviving comrades before the battle; it is Launcelot who brings Guenevere to life for us 'in the old garden days'; and we ride helplessly with her 'along the dripping, leafless woods', anticipating the slaughter and betrayal 'beside the haystack in the floods'. This ability to relive and revitalize the past is characteristic of all Morris's creative work, and is as evident in his approach to design as it is in his writing. He was, of course, selective in his choice of subjects from the past, and his undergraduate preoccupation with themes from Malory's *Morte d'Arthur* was to be replaced with an obsession with Nordic myths and legends, and finally with the 'people's' past (and future). His 'Socialist' writing, however, is as vivid and evocative as his early work, so that *A Dream of John Ball*, first serialized in *The Commonweal* in 1886, shares the same qualities as *The Early Romances*, presenting the characters and events of the Peasants' Revolt with a similar immediacy; and, as in the *Romances*, the sense of continuity from the fourteenth to the nineteenth century is evoked through descriptions of the familiar landscape and buildings of Kent, just as in *News from Nowhere* the London of the twenty-first century, although transformed by sweetness and light, is still recognizable by its landmarks: buildings and places that remind the narrator of grimmer times.

In spite of these very obvious gifts of evocation, Morris's characters remain stereotyped: they follow the 'romance' convention of the personification of good and evil, betrayer and betrayed, and this is most evident in his descriptions of women. For although he is able to enter into and thus convey the anguish of Guenevere, she is set apart as much by her beauty as by her shame, and 'Praise of My Lady', his first poem in homage to a real rather than legendary woman, describes an ideal of womanhood, rather than the reality of Jane Burden. Morris's love, therefore, and his hopes for love, were also 'the embodiment of dreams' in these early years.

Apart from this poem, and hints in other early poems, there are no available or surviving letters from William Morris describing his obsession with Jane's beauty, or their courtship and marriage, so we have to rely on the accounts of others for this aspect of his life. According to Mackail, it was Burne-Jones and Rossetti, both in Oxford to work on the Union murals, who first saw this 'remarkable beauty, of a type not common in England'. She was at the theatre with her sister Bessy ('an accidental person', according to Morris, who seemed to hover round their lives, featureless and characterless, doing a little embroidery now and then); the painters recognized Jane as 'a stunner', made her acquaintance, and persuaded her to sit for them. And so she met and married 'the dreamer of dreams'. Morris was then 25 and she was 18. Swinburne, the poet, said that he liked to think of Morris 'having that wonderful and most perfect stunner of his – to look at or speak to. The idea of his marrying

her is insane. To kiss her feet is the utmost men should dream of doing.' What the Morris family thought of the marriage is unrecorded, for William had obviously married 'out of his class', for love rather than for money or status, and in doing so had further identified himself in his mother's eyes with the Bohemian world of painters and poets.

It is very obvious, however, from Morris's letter to his mother (pages 25–7) breaking the news that he had definitely decided to become an architect, that he needed to validate his actions according to his own principles. His mother had evidently reminded him of the money spent on sending him to Oxford, and of the evil of idleness (an accusation that could scarcely apply to her eldest son, who was hyperactive in his energies, and who could never bear the thought of sitting still). To Mrs Morris, however, work had to be consistent, as well as deemed worthy, and William had to persuade her that his chosen profession was a serious one. It would be good for him, he explained, to have to do what he was told for the proposed three-years' apprenticeship; architecture was a trade, and would earn him an adequate living; but above all he would be happy in the work: '. . . I do not hope to be great at all in anything, but perhaps I may reasonably hope to be happy in my work, and sometimes when I am idle and doing nothing, pleasant visions go past me of the things that may be . . .'

The need for work to be a pleasure rather than a duty or a curse was, of course, central to Morris's thinking throughout his life. At the same time, however, his decision to become an architect rather than a priest (or a stockbroker like his father) was based on more complex reasons than he admitted, at least to his mother. In the first place he had loved and studied buildings since his childhood, with an interest that was rational as well as emotional. He had read about buildings as well as looked at them. He knew when and how they were built, how the carvers and decorators worked, how the stones and their different textures weathered with age, and how they had been added to or altered by successive generations. This enthusiasm was transformed into commitment when he was at Oxford, and went on his pilgrimages to the northern French cathedrals. It was his experience of Chartres, Amiens and, above all, 'the mingled beauty, history and romance' of Rouen that convinced him that he must become an architect. This was living history, a demonstration of the ideals and achievements of the past, achievements that were popular as well as heroic. But at the same time it was a past threatened by the present, so that the preservation and continuation of the traditions and values symbolized by such architecture became a cause and a crusade for Morris. Such traditions might be recalled in paintings, poetry and stories, as well as in polemics, but could not be recreated. Architecture, on the other hand, was reality; it was a demonstration of the history of human values.

Morris, no doubt, had always assumed this, but such convictions were confirmed by the persuasive writings of John Ruskin. Ruskin had published *The Seven Lamps of Architecture*, with its demand for morality in architecture, in 1849; his *Stones of Venice* was published in two volumes in 1851 and 1853, and it was one chapter in the second of these volumes that caught Morris's attention, as well as that of many of his contemporaries. 'On the Nature of Gothic', a text vital to the understanding of English attitudes to design and architecture from the 1850s onwards, is based on the assumption that cultural values are reflected in the art, artefacts and buildings of any given society. This, of course, was not a new idea, and Ruskin's championship of Gothic or medieval architecture was also shared by many others in the mid-nineteenth century. Ruskin, however, added a moral dimension to these debates by his demonstration of the intrinsic *humanism* of the Gothic: 'The Greek', according to Ruskin, 'gave to the lower workmen no subject which he could not perfectly execute. The Assyrian gave him subjects which he could only execute imperfectly, but fixed a legal standard for his imperfection. The workman was, in both systems, a slave. But in the mediaeval, or especially Christian system of ornament, this slavery was done away with altogether; Christianity having recognized, in small things as well as great, the individual value of every soul. But it not only recognizes its value; it confesses its imperfection.'

According to Ruskin, architecture and its attendant arts were to be judged according to the amount of freedom of expression they allowed to the workman; perfection and precision were suspect since they implied direction, and therefore repression, and the Christian humanism that had inspired Gothic architecture, from cottages to cathedrals, also ensured a humane and caring, as well as a free and creative society. Ruskin, therefore, was a social critic as well as an interpreter of the nature of style, and he used the values he associated with Gothic to castigate the fundamental immorality of contemporary society, which gave the workman less freedom than in any previous age. The introduction of machinery and mechanization had totally destroyed any humanism implicit in English traditions of social order, and this destruction was reflected in a factory system which debased both product and producer: '. . . And the great cry that rises from all our manufacturing cities, louder than their furnace blast, is in all in very deed for this, – that we manufacture everything there except men; we blanch cotton, strengthen steel, and refine sugar, and shape pottery; but to brighten, to strengthen, to refine or to form a single living spirit never enters into our estimate of advantages.'

Morris reprinted 'On the Nature of Gothic' at the Kelmscott Press in 1892, describing it as 'one of the very few necessary and inevitable utterances of the century'. 'To some of us when we first read it,' he wrote, '. . . it seemed to point out a new road on which the world should travel.'

By choosing architecture as a profession, therefore, Morris was choosing commitment. He apprenticed himself to the architect G.E. Street in the hope of doing work that was socially justifiable as well as enjoyable. 'Looking like a wonderful bird just out of its shell' (according to the young Philip Webb, who was also working for Street, and who was to become Morris's life-long friend), he applied himself with his customary vigour. In this case, however, application did not lead to perfection, and Morris, then under the spell of the charismatic Rossetti, decided to become a painter, with equal lack of success. And although he continued writing during this period, as well as experimenting with stone and wood-carving, and ill-uminating, his mother might well have been justified in accusing him of dilettantism. Her son had neither a vocation nor a trade – he spent his time scribbling poetry, and his money buying paintings and filling the rooms he shared with Burne-Jones with ridiculous furniture. Moreover, he had married a wife who had only her beauty to recommend her.

Morris, however, was still preoccupied with the realization of his ideal world, which at this stage was entirely personal to him (and his friends). Philip Webb built him the beautiful Red House ('our palace of Art'), so different from the homes of his childhood. According to Rossetti, it was 'More a poem than a house, but admirable to live in too'. With its high-pitched and irregular roof-lines, its half-hipped gables and arched doorways, it shows little evidence of labour at the drawing board; it aspires to an ideal of the vernacular, and seems to have grown there, like the trees in the apple-orchard in which it was built. Apart from his somewhat laconic account in his letter to Andreas Scheu ('I . . . got a friend to build me a house very medieval in spirit in which I lived for five years, and set myself to decorating it'), there is little in Morris's writing about this period in his life. The house, therefore, its furniture and decoration, and his friends' descriptions of the hospitality there, must speak for his aspirations at this time. Both his children were born at Red House, and the 'Fine Art Workmen' enterprise was established there, so that Morris at last had a 'trade' to serve as a focus for his energies. He also began to write his 'Big Book' at Red House, *The Earthly Paradise*, which was to establish his reputa-tion as a poet. *The Earthly Paradise* was begun in the spirit of Chaucer, and was a re-telling of most of the classic myths and legends. But during the course of writing it, Morris's personal idyll was shattered: part-ly because of the success of the 'Firm' he was forced to abandon Red House and move back to London; and at the same time his marriage was failing, and although he had 'a head always fit for Launcelot or Tristram', he was, in fact, playing the role of King Arthur or King Mark, and losing his Guenevere/Isolde to his erst-while hero and friend, Rossetti.

This was the blackest period of Morris's personal life, but the only evidence at present available of what he was feeling then is 'concealed' in the prologues to the later tales in *The Earthly Paradise*, and in some poetry that was not published in his lifetime. He had no wish, however, to remain forever 'Like a new-wakened man . . . who tries to dream again the dream that made him glad' ('September'); he had his work, designing as well as writing, he had his friends, and he felt himself responsible for the happiness of his fami-ly. He does not blame, reproach or diminish Janey in any of his published writing (although Rossetti is ob-viously an irritant); he does his best to support her emotionally as well as financially, tending her in her illnesses, and leasing Kelmscott Manor so that she and Rossetti could be together. He had further cause for grief and anxiety in 1876, when his elder daughter Jenny was diagnosed as epileptic, and his concern for the welfare and happiness of the trio is evident in all his letters to them. (Many of Morris's biographers maintain that Morris may have felt himself in part responsible for Jenny's illness, his own violent rages perhaps indicating some hereditary instability.) Implicit in his surviving correspondence with his wife is Morris's determination that she should feel no guilt ('Janey, be happy'); Janey and the children shared his interest in the work of the 'Firm' and in politics, and when he is not with them, he writes to them about his professional life, their mutual friends, and even the weather. (This traditional conversational stand-by of the English was a very real concern with Morris, and entries in his surviving diaries give detailed daily ac-counts of wind-direction, rainfall, mist, fog and sun-shine.) He rarely mentions the weather, however, when he is writing to Aglaia Coronio or Georgiana Burne-Jones; these two women became his confi-dantes, and Georgiana (who had her own problems with the impressionable Edward and his involvements with beautiful women) had a special place in his heart. It is to her that he addresses his most intimate thoughts, and it is to her that he dedicates the exquisite *Book of Verse* which he helped to illuminate, and which reminded him of the delights of pattern-making.

It was during these times of personal crisis, when it

became obvious that the Earthly Paradise was not to be found in family life in a palace of art, that the implications of Morris's work and writing became more profound. As the documentation presented here shows, this was also a period of intensive activity for Morris: he made his first expedition to Iceland in 1871; he began his collaboration with Thomas Wardle in 1875; he became involved with the Eastern Question Association in 1876, and he was active in the formation of The Society for the Protection of Ancient Buildings in 1877. These were not, however, disparate and disconnected enthusiasms; they were the logical and inevitable outcome of his earlier preoccupations, and they were all part of Morris's quest for what he was later to call 'the new order of things'.

He had become interested in the Nordic sagas when he was writing *The Earthly Paradise*, and he learned Icelandic so that he could read them in the original as well as translate them. His fascination with these northern myths formed part of his search for a personal as well as a 'folk' identity that he had, perhaps, found lacking in the legends of Greece and Rome. (Wagner, of course, anticipated and shared these preoccupations; Morris, however, who seems to have had little time for modern music, especially opera, declared Wagner's 'theories on musical matters perfectly abhominable' [sic], and was appalled by 'the idea of a sandy-haired German tenor tweedledeeing over the unspeakable woes of Sigurd'.) Morris's interest in northern legends, however, was prompted by a search for a northern European as opposed to a national past, jingoism in all its forms being equally abhorrent to him. In Iceland he found the landscape as well as the values of the mythic past surviving in a relentless environment that made mockery of conventional views of 'progress'. ('I learned one lesson there, thoroughly I hope', he was to tell his socialist colleague, Andreas Scheu, 'that the most grinding poverty is a trifling evil compared with the inequality of the classes.')

Morris was beginning to realize the true meaning of the 'lessons' he had learned in the past. His collaboration with Thomas Wardle, and the fury he felt at the incompetence and seeming indifference of the work-

men at Leek confirmed all that he had read in Ruskin: that industrialization and the division of labour destroyed pride, as well as joy in work. Equally, the so-called 'restoration' of ancient buildings was a desecration of the people's past, the destruction of 'a popular art', as Morris put it – an art that was living history – not the text-book accounts of great kings and warriors, but of the anonymous achievements of the people. When Morris considered the people's past, it was not the selective past of one specific country; it was a collective past that had contributed to the creation of a vernacular of excellence, a common language of art and beauty that still survived in some parts of Europe, Asia and India, but which was now threatened or destroyed by the demands of commerce and profit-mongering. So it was inevitable that William Morris, once stung into political involvement, should identify himself with the people's cause and, like his contemporary Karl Marx, see the war between capital and labour as the major issue in contemporary society. There was no sudden conversion, and no violent transition between Morris the Romantic and Morris the Revolutionary; he was consistent in all his thinking, in his theory as well as his practice, always relating his ideals and interpretation of the past to his hopes and fears for the future.

Morris's personal ideals for art are demonstrated in the illustrations selected for this book. His work is breathtakingly beautiful, and his designs, which have the inevitability of natural growth, are the result of observation and obsession: observation of nature, and the colours and forms of nature; observation of the responses to pattern-making in various cultures; and an obsession with perfection, whatever the cost. His methods of work and the standards he required from himself and those who worked with him are clearly set out in his correspondence with Thomas Wardle. He knew exactly what he wanted, and he was never satisfied with compromise. As one of his contemporaries put it: 'His work will necessarily remain supreme until as great a man as Morris again deals with that manner of expression with his *full force* as he did.' When he began to lecture about his work in the late 1870s he spelled out his ideals to his audiences:

'...nothing can be a work of art that is not useful...';
'...never forget the material you are working with, and try always to use it for what it can do best...';
'...everything made by man's hands has a form, which must be either beautiful or ugly; beautiful if it is in accord with Nature, and helps her; ugly if it is discordant with nature, and thwarts her; it cannot be indifferent...'

Indifference was not one of the qualities Morris promoted or inspired, either in his life-time or subsequently. According to E. P. Thompson, William Morris was and is 'one of those men whom history will never overtake'; his work and his social commitment inspired a generation of designers in Europe and America to attempt, by means of design and architecture, to make the world a better place to live in. It is significant, however, that Morris himself came to despair of survival through design, and that once he was fully committed to socialism he designed very little himself, and left the practical work and administration of the Firm to others. (The Kelmscott Press, his final great achievement, was also his final, perhaps his only, self-indulgence.) For Morris realized that the society he hoped for was unattainable without some form of social revolution, and in *News from Nowhere*, his last 'romance', the Utopian society he describes was founded in the aftermath of a bitter civil, and therefore class, war. Nor did he find his encounters with 'professional' socialists particularly encouraging. The 'politics' of politicians appalled him, although he himself always remained true to his own interpretation of the workers' cause: he was an honest man seeking to promote honest ideals, and if the extracts quoted in this book demonstrate anything, they

demonstrate this. The selection, of course, is inevitably inadequate: William Morris wrote so much and achieved so much that it is impossible to convey the breadth and scope of his endeavours in one volume. But it is to be hoped that the book does convey something of the man that he was, as well as his achievements.

But although *William Morris by Himself* is, of course, intended to be by Morris rather than about him, it is interesting to speculate about his possible reactions to today's consumer society, so different from the idyll he presented in *News from Nowhere*. Wars as well as revolutions have shattered the world he knew; they have not produced an ideal society, and the problem of survival is even more urgent. To many of us, however, more or less secure in our pleasant homes (many of them, no doubt, delightfully furnished with designs by Morris), survival is for others less fortunate than ourselves. William Morris would have no time for us; nor would he, in all probability, have much time for art and design in the age of multinational enterprises and mass consumption. He would, however, have been concerned for the future of our common inheritance – the earth he loved so deeply, the rivers and the countryside, the forests and the flowers, and he would also have been concerned for those too helpless to help themselves. The earth, he would tell us, is not ours to destroy: it belongs to the past as well as to the future of all of us, and it is our responsibility. Responsibility, on a personal as well as a public level, was something William Morris took very seriously. And he would be trying, by all the means within his power, to make the rest of humanity share his concern.

MY VERY UNEVENTFUL LIFE

5 SEPT. 1883

To Andreas Scheu   I was born at Walthamstow in Essex in March 1834, a suburban village on the edge of Epping Forest, and once a pleasant place enough, but now terribly cocknified and choked up by the jerry-builder.

My Father was a business man in the city, and well-to-do; and we lived in the ordinary bourgeois style of comfort; and since we belonged to the evangelical section of the English Church I was brought up in what I should call rich establishmentarian puritanism; a religion which even as a boy I never took to.

I went to school at Marlborough College, which was then a new and very rough school. As far as my school instruction went, I think I may fairly say I learned next to nothing there, for indeed next to nothing was taught; but the place is in very beautiful country, thickly scattered over with prehistoric monuments, and I set myself eagerly to studying these and everything else that had any history in it, and so perhaps learned a good deal, especially as there was a good library at the school to which I sometimes had access. I should mention that ever since I could remember I was a great devourer of books. I don't remember being taught to read, and by the time I was 7 years old I had read a very great many books good, bad and indifferent.

My Father died in 1847 a few months before I went to Marlborough; but as he had engaged in a fortunate mining speculation before his death, we were left very well off, rich in fact.

I went to Oxford in 1853 as a member of Exeter College; I took very ill to the studies of the place; but fell to very vigorously on history and especially mediaeval history, all the more perhaps because at this time I fell under the influence of the High Church or Puseyite school; this latter phase however did not last me long, as it was corrected by the books of John Ruskin which were at the time a sort of revelation to me; I was also a good deal influenced by the works of Charles Kingsley, and got into my head therefrom some sociopolitical ideas which would have developed probably but for the attractions of art and poetry. While I was still an undergraduate, I discovered that I could write poetry, much to my own amazement; and about that time being very intimate with other young men of enthusiastic ideas, we got up a monthly paper which lasted (to my cost) for a year; it was called the *Oxford and Cambridge Magazine*, and was very *young* indeed. When I had gone through my schools at Oxford, I who had been originally intended for the Church!!! made up my mind to take to art in some form, and so articled myself to G.E. Street (the architect of the new Law Courts afterwards) who was then practising in Oxford; I only stayed with him nine months however; when being in London and having been introduced by Burne-Jones, the painter, who was my great college friend, to Dante Gabriel Rossetti, the leader of the Pre-Raphaelite School, I made up my mind to turn painter, and studied the art but in a very desultory way for some time.

At this time the revival of Gothic architecture was making great progress in England and naturally touched the Pre-Raphaelite movement also; I threw myself into these movements with all my heart: got a friend to build me a house very mediæval in spirit in which I lived for 5 years, and set myself to decorating it; we found, I and my friend the architect especially, that all the minor arts were in a state of complete degradation especially in England, and accordingly in 1861 with the conceited courage of a young man I set myself to reforming all that: and started a sort of firm for producing decorative articles. D.G. Rossetti, Ford Madox Brown, Burne-Jones and P. Webb the architect of my house were the chief members of it as far as designing went. Burne-Jones was beginning to have a reputation at that time; he did a great many designs for us for stained glass, and entered very heartily into the matter; and we made some progress before long, though we were naturally much ridiculed. I took the matter up as a business and began in the teeth of difficulties not easy to imagine to make some money in it: about ten years ago the firm broke up, leaving me the only partner, though I still receive help and designs from P. Webb and Burne-Jones.

Meantime in 1858 I published a volume of poems *The Defence of Guenevere*; exceedingly young also and very mediæval; and then after a lapse of some years conceived the idea of my *Earthly Paradise*, and fell to work very hard at it. I had about this time extended my historical reading by falling in with translations from the old Norse literature, and found it a good corrective to the maundering side of mediaevalism. In 1866 (I think) I published the *Life and Death of Jason*, which, originally intended for one of the tales of the *Earthly Paradise*, had got too long for the purpose. To my surprise the book was very well received both by reviewers and the public, who were kinder still to my next work, *The Earthly Paradise*, the first series of which I published in 1868. In 1872 I published a fantastic little book chiefly lyrical called *Love is Enough*. Meantime about 1870 I had made the acquaintance of an Icelandic gentleman, Mr E. Magnússon, of whom I learned to read the language of the North, and with whom I studied most of the works of that literature; the delightful freshness and independence of thought of them, the air of freedom which breathes through them, their worship of courage (the great virtue of the human race), their utter unconventionality took my heart by storm. I translated with Mr Magnússon's help, and published, *The Story of Grettir the Strong*, a set of Sagas (about 6) under the title of *Northern Love Stories*, and finally the Icelandic version of the *Nibelung Tale*, called the *Volsunga Saga*.

In 1871 I went to Iceland with Mr Magnússon, and, apart from my pleasure in seeing that romantic desert, I learned one lesson there, thoroughly I hope, that the most grinding poverty is a trifling evil compared with the inequality of classes. In 1873 I went to Iceland again. In 1876 I published a translation of the *Æneid of Virgil*, which was fairly well received. In 1877 I began my last poem, an Epic of the Niblung Story founded chiefly on the Icelandic version. I published this in 1878 under the title of *Sigurd the Volsung and the Fall of the Niblungs*.

Through all this time I have been working hard at my business, in which I have had a considerable success even from the commercial side; I believe that if I had yielded on a few points of principle I might have become a positively rich man; but even as it is I have nothing to complain of, although the last few years have been so slack in business.

Almost all the designs we use for surface decoration, wallpapers, textiles, and the like, I design myself. I have had to learn the theory and to some extent the practice of weaving, dyeing, & textile printing: all of which I must admit has given me and still gives me a great deal of enjoyment.

But in spite of all the success I have had, I have not failed to be conscious that the art I have been helping to produce would fall with the death of a few of us who really care about it, that a reform in art which is founded on individualism must perish with the individuals who have set it going. Both my historical studies and my practical conflict with the philistinism of modern society have *forced* on me the conviction that art cannot have a real life and growth under the present system of commercialism and profit-mongering. I have tried to develop this view, which is in fact Socialism seen through the eyes of an artist, in various lectures, the first of which I delivered in 1878.

About the time when I was beginning to think so strongly on these points that I felt I must express myself publicly, came the crisis of the Eastern Question and the agitation which ended in the overthrow of the Disraeli government. I joined heartily in that agitation on the Liberal side, because it seemed to me that England risked drifting into a war which would have committed her to the party of reaction: I also thoroughly dreaded the outburst of Chauvinism which swept over the country, and feared that once we were amusing ourselves with an European war no one in this country would listen to anything of social questions; nor could I see in England at any time any party more advanced than the Radicals, who were also it must be remembered hallowed as it were by being in opposition to the party which openly proclaimed themselves reactionists; I was under small illusion as to the result of a victory of the Liberals, except so far as it would stem the torrent of Chauvinism, and check the feeling of national hatred and prejudice for which I shall always feel the most profound contempt. I therefore took an active part in the anti-Turk agitation, was a member of the committee of the Eastern Question Association, and worked hard at it; I made the acquaintance of some of the Trades Union leaders at the time; but found that they were quite under the influence of the Capitalist politicians, and that, the General Election once gained, they would take no forward step whatever. The action and want of action of the new Liberal Parliament, especially the Coercion Bill and the Stockjob-ber's Egyptian War, quite destroyed any hope I might have had of any good being done by alliance with the Radical party, however advanced they might call themselves.

I joined a committee (of which Mr Herbert Burrows was Secretary) which tried to stir up some opposition to the course the Liberal government and party were taking in the early days of this parliament; but it speedily fell to pieces, having in fact no sort of practical principles to hold it together; I mention this to show that I was on the look out for joining any body which seemed likely to push forward matters.

It must be understood that I always intended to join any body who distinctly called them-selves socialists, so when last year I was invited to join the Democratic Federation by Mr Hyndman, I accepted the invitation hoping that it would declare for Socialism, in spite of certain drawbacks that I expected to find in it; concerning which I find on the whole that there are fewer drawbacks than I expected.

I should have written above that I married in 1859 and have two daughters by that marriage very sympathetic with me as to my aims in life.

DREAMER OF DREAMS

When I was a boy . . .

William Morris was the privileged child of prosperous middle-class parents. His father had made a considerable fortune by investing in a Devonshire copper mining company, and in the 1830s he and his wife and two small daughters had moved to Walthamstow, the 'suburban village on the edge of Epping Forest'. They first lived at Elm House, where William was born – he was the first of five sons and he had two more sisters – and in 1840, when he was six, the family moved to Woodford Hall, a large mansion with extensive grounds. There Morris seems to have enjoyed an idyllic childhood; the children had ponies, they explored their own 'primeval' forest, and William was given a diminutive suit of armour so that he could indulge his fantasies about medieval knights and their doughty deeds.

When Morris was thirteen his father died, and although he never refers to this early bereavement in letters and reminiscences, he did remember a visit he made with his father to Canterbury Cathedral – he was eight years old at the time and thought that 'the gates of heaven had opened'. Morris Senior's death made no difference to the family's fortunes, although they left the palatial Woodford Hall and moved to Water House in Walthamstow – now the William Morris Gallery.

Both J.W. Mackail, Morris's first biographer, and his daughter May Morris draw on William's own memories of his childhood in their books, and from his writing it is also possible to catch glimpses of what his life was like then, and what remained precious to him. The 'primeval' forests are evoked again and again in his poetry and in his stories, as are the surrounding churches and villages: '. . . the old Essex churches and their brasses were known by Morris at a very early age . . .' writes Mackail. And Proust-like, certain scents and flowers would evoke that distant world: 'To this day when I smell a may-tree I think of going to bed in day-light.'

WOODFORD HALL, ESSEX

From News from Nowhere   . . . one of the girls, the handsome one, who had been scattering little twigs of lavender and other sweet-smelling herbs about the floor, came near to listen, and stood behind me with her hand on my shoulder, in which she held some of the plant I used to call balm: its strong, sweet smell brought back to my mind the very early days in the kitchen garden at Woodford, and the large blue plums which grew on the wall beyond the sweet-herb patch, — a connection of memories which all boys will see at once.

15 NOV. 1874

To Louisa Baldwin   . . . I used to dread Sundays when I was a little chap . . .

From J.W. Mackail, The Life of William Morris   '. . . I remember being taught to spell and standing on a chair with my shoes off because I made so many mistakes . . .'

KELMSCOTT HOUSE, 23 DEC. 1888

To Jenny [daughter]   By the way I did intend to give you some information about the *stocks* in my last and it somehow slipped out of my memory. When we lived at Woodford there were stocks there on a little bit of wayside green in the middle of the village: beside them stood the *cage*, a small shanty some 12 ft sq: and it was built of brown brick roofed with blue slate. I suppose it had been quite recently in use since its *style* was not earlier than the days of fat George. I remember that I used to look at the two threats of law and order with considerable terror, and decidedly preferred to walk on the opposite side of the road; but I never heard of anybody being locked up in the cage or laid by the heels in the stocks . . .

From 'The Lesser Arts of Life' [lecture, 1882]   How well I remember as a boy my first acquaintance with a room hung with faded greenery at Queen Elizabeth's Lodge, by Chingford Hatch, in Epping Forest . . . and the impression of romance that it made upon me; a feeling that always comes back on me when I read, as I often do, Sir Walter Scott's Antiquary, and come to the description of the green room at Monkbarns, amongst which the novelist has with such exquisite cunning of art imbedded the fresh and glittering verses of the summer poet Chaucer; yes, that was more than upholstery, believe me.

From 'Frank's Sealed Letter'   . . . I was in the country soon: people called it an ugly country, I knew, that spreading of the broad marsh lands round the river Lea; but I was so weary with my hard work that it seemed very lovely to me then; indeed, I think I should not have despised it at any time. I was always a lover of the sad lowlands country . . . Ah! such thoughts of the old times came about me thronging . . . I noticed every turn of the banks of the little brook, every ripple of its waters over the brown stones, every line of the broad-leaved waterflowers; I went down towards the brook, and, stooping down, gathered a knot of lush marsh-marigolds; then, kneeling on both knees, bent over the water with my arm stretched down to it, till both my hand and the yellow flowers were making the swift running little stream bubble about them . . . Ah! what was it all, that picture of the old past days.

I see a little girl sitting on the grass, beneath the limes in the hot summertide, with eyes fixed on the far away blue hills, and seeing who knows what shapes there; for the boy by her side is reading to her wondrous stories of knight and lady, and fairy thing, that lived in the ancient days . . .

UNDATED (PROBABLY 1886 or 1887)

To the Rev. William Sharman   . . . my parents did as all right people do, shook off the responsibility of my education as soon as they could; handing me over first to nurses, then to grooms and gardeners, and then to a school – a boy-farm, I should say. In one way or another I learned chiefly one thing from all these – rebellion.

MARLBRO' COLLEGE, 1 NOV. 1848

To Emma [sister]   . . . Things go on much in the same way as usual – three new prefects are going to be made in the next few days. Today being a Saints Day I am one to be chatechized in Evening Service as I was also catechized last Sunday; these last two or three days it has been very misty and dark indeed, the gates are shut now at 5 o'clock and the lamps are lighted at the same time. . . . I think the winter is regularly coming on now, the trees are getting very bare indeed now about here, it is now only 7 weeks to the Holidays, there I go again! I am sure you think me a great fool to be always thinking about home always, but I really can't help it I don't think it is my fault for there are such a lot of things I want to do and say, and see, but I can't write any more now so best love to all . . .

MARLBRO' COLLEGE, 13 APRIL 1849

. . . On Monday I went to Silbury Hill which I think I have told you before is an artificial hill made by the Britons but first I went to a place called Abury [Avebury] where there is a Druidical circle and a Roman entrenchment both which encircle the town   originally it is supposed that the stones were in this shape: first one large circle then a smaller one inside this and then one in the middle for an altar but a great many, in fact *most* of the stones have been removed so I could [not] tell this   on Tuesday Morning I was told of this so I thought I would go there again, I did and then I was able to understand how they had been fixed; I think the biggest stone I could see had about 16 feet out of the ground in height and about 10 ft thick and 12 ft broad   the circle and entrenchment altogether is about ½ a mile; at Abury I also saw a very old church   the tower was very pretty indeed   it had four little spires on it of the decorated order and there was a little Porch and inside the porch a beautiful Norman doorway loaded with mouldings   the chancel was new and was paved with tesselated pavement   this I saw through the window for I did not know where the sexton's house was, so of course I could not get the key, There was a pretty little Parsonage house close by the church. After we had done looking at the lions of Abury, which took us about ½ an hour we went through a *mud lane* down one or two water fields and *last* but not *least* through what they call here a *water meadow* up to our knees in water, now perhaps you do not know what a water meadow is as there are none of them in your part of the world   So for your edification, I will tell you what a delectable

A VIEW OF AVEBURY, WILTSHIRE

affair a water meadow is to go through; in the first place you must fancy a field cut through with an infinity of small streams say about four feet wide each   the people to whom the meadow belongs can turn these streams on and off when they like and at this time of the year they are on just before they put the fields up for mowing   the grass being very long you cannot see the water till you are in the water and floundering in it except you are in above the field.   luckily the water had not been bog when we went through it else we should have been up to our middles in mud, however perhaps now you can imagine a water meadow: after we had scrambled through this meadow we ascended Silbury Hill   it is not very high but yet I should think it must have taken an immense long time to have got it together   I brought away a little white snail shell as a memento of the place and have got it in my pocket book . . .

DEC. 1874

To Philip Burne-Jones   . . . Did you ever see my old room in A House – I thought it such a dismal place when I looked in there the other day – a troublous life I led of it there for two years, after which I became a dignified person comparatively and was Captain of the room: are there still Captains of dormitorys?

Alas I did not fight enough in my time, from want of hope let us say, not want of courage, or else I should have been more respected in my earlier days: in the few fights I had I was rather successful, for a little, and thin (yes) boy as I was: for the rest I had a hardish time of it, as chaps who have brains and feelings generally do at school, or say in all the world even, whose griefs are not much shared in by the hard and stupid: nor its joys either, happily, so that we may be well content to be alive and eager, and to bear pain sometimes rather than to grow like rotting cabbages and not to mind it.

A hint to you on the mechanical part of battle: I was watching two little boys fighting in the street and it refreshed my memory of what used to go on at school: for each seemed afraid of the other and held his head down and hit round; and certainly the one who had stood up straight and hit out well from the shoulder would have got the best of it: and you may take as a certain rule both in fisticuffs and all manner of fighting that if you are not afraid of being hit you can hit your enemy, and then the rest is a matter of endurance only . . .

. . . Nothing that has happened to me since I was at school has given me quite as much pleasure as coming home for the holidays: make up your mind to that Phil, you will never be as happy again as you will be tomorrow week – though I hope with all my heart that you will always be very happy and my good friend . . .

A vision of grey-roofed houses and the sound of many bells

Morris went up to Exeter College, Oxford in 1853, ostensibly to study for the clergy. The first of the many friends he made there was Edward Burne-Jones, and through him he met Charles Faulkner and Cormell Price (Crom). They read poetry together (Tennyson, Keats and Shelley), novels (Kingsley, Thackeray and Dickens) and, above all, Ruskin. They resolved to form a Brotherhood, and to mount 'A Crusade and Holy Warfare against this age'. In 1855 they launched the Oxford and Cambridge Magazine, *which was financed by Morris, and which ran for a year. Morris's early writing was published in the magazine, and his discovery of poetry, together with his enthusiasm for architecture, revitalized by his visits to the cathedrals of northern France, convinced him that he was not meant to be a clergyman.*

SELF-PORTRAIT, *c.* 1855

From A Dream of John Ball   'Hast thou seen Oxford, scholar?'

A vision of grey-roofed houses and a long-winding street and the sound of many bells came over me at that word . . .

From News from Nowhere

Sunset was in the sky as we skirted Oxford by Oseney. . . It was a matter of course that so far as they could be seen from the river, I missed none of the towers and spires of that once don-beridden city; but the meadows all round, which, when I had last passed through them, were getting daily more and more squalid, more and more impressed with the seal of the 'stir and intellectual life of the nineteenth century' were no longer intellectual, but had once again become as beautiful as they should be, and the little hill of Hinksey, with two or three very pretty stone houses new-grown on it (I use the word advisedly; for they seemed to belong to it) looked down happily on the full streams and waving grass, grey now, but for the sunset, with its fast-ripening seeds.

WALTHAMSTOW, APRIL 1855

To Cormell Price

. . . I have read a little Shelley since I saw you last; I like it very much what I have read: 'The Skylark' was one: WHAT a gorgeous thing it is! Utterly different from anything else. . . . I hope I shall be able to make you understand what I mean, for I am a sad muddle-head: I mean that most beautiful poetry, and indeed almost all beautiful writing makes one feel sad, or indignant, or – do you understand, for I can't make it any clearer; but 'The Skylark' makes one feel happy only; I suppose because it is nearly all music, and that it doesn't bring up any thoughts of humanity: but I don't know either . . .

WALTHAMSTOW, JULY 1855

. . . I have finished the tale I began last term [probably 'The Story of the Unknown Church'] and failed singularly therein, I'm afraid it won't do for the Brotherhood. . .

. . . As to Cambridge, it is rather a hole of a place, and can't compare for a moment with Oxford; it is such a very different kind of place too, that one feels inclined to laugh, at least I do, when I think of it. I suppose by this time Ted has told you all about it, and how we went to see Ely, which disappointed me somewhat, it is so horribly spoilt with very well meant restorations, as they facetiously call them . . .

AVRANCHES, NORMANDY, 10 AUG. 1855

. . . O! the glories of the Churches we have seen! Crom, we have seen nine Cathedrals, and let me see how many non-Cathedral Churches; I must count them on my fingers; there, I think I have missed some but I have made out 24 all splendid Churches; some of them surpassing first-rate English Cathedrals.

. . . Behold our itinerary. We started from Chartres quite early (six o'clock) with drizzling rain that almost hid the spires of the Cathedral, how splendid they looked in the midst of it! but we were obliged to leave them, and the beautiful statues, and the stained glass, and the great, cliff-like buttresses, for quite a long time I'm afraid – so we went for about 20 miles by railroad to a place called Maintenon, where we mounted the quaint little conveyance and went off, with the rain still falling a little, through the beautiful country to Dreux, for a distance of about 17 miles; there was plenty to look at by the road, I almost think I like that part of the country better than any other part of the lovely country we have seen in France; so gloriously the trees are grouped, all manner of trees, but more especially the graceful poplars and aspens, of all kinds; and the hedgeless fields of grain, and beautiful herbs that they grow for forage whose names I don't know, the most beautiful fields I ever saw yet . . . Well, we had to stop at Dreux about an hour and we saw the church there, a very good one, flamboyant mostly, but with an earlier apse very evilly used, and with a transept front very elaborately carved once, now very forlorn and battered, but (Deo gratias) not yet restored: there is a delightful old secular tower at Dreux too, and that is flamboyant also, with a roof like the side of a cliff, it is so steep. . . . We had only a very short time to stay at Evreux, and even that short time we had to divide (alas! for our Lower Nature) between eating our dinner and gazing on the gorgeous Cathedral: it is an exceedingly lovely one, though not nearly so large as most of the Cathedrals we saw, the aisles are very rich flamboyant, with a great deal of light canopy work about them; the rest of the Church is earlier, the nave being Norman, and the choir fully developed early Gothic; though the transepts and lantern are flamboyant also by the way: there is a great deal of good stained glass about the Church. . . . at last we got to Louviers; there is a splendid church there, though it is not a large one; the outside has a kind of mask of the most gorgeous flamboyant (though late) thrown all over it, with such parapets and windows, it is so gorgeous and light, that I was utterly unprepared for the inside, and almost startled by it; so solemn it looked and calm after the fierce flamboyant of the outside; for all the interior, except the Chapels, is quite early Gothic and very beautiful; I have never, either before or since, been so much struck with the difference between the early and late Gothic, and by the greater nobleness of the former. . . . O! the trees! it was all like the country in a beautiful poem, in a beautiful Romance such as might make a background to Chaucer's Palamon and Arcite; how we could see the valley winding away along the side of the Eure a long way, under the hills: but we had to leave it and go to Rouen by a nasty, brimstone, noisy, shrieking railway train that cares not twopence for hill or valley, poplar tree or lime tree, corn poppy or blue cornflower, or purple thistle and purple vetch, white convolvulus, white clematis, or golden S. John's wort; that cares not twopence either for tower, or spire, or apse, or dome, till it will be as noisy and obtrusive under the spires of Chartres or the towers of Rouen, as it is [under] Versailles or the Dome of the Invalides; verily railways are ABOMINATIONS; and I think I have never fairly realised this fact till this our tour . . .

From 'The Aims of Art' [lecture, 1887]   . . . Less than forty years ago – about thirty – I first saw the city of Rouen, then still in its outward aspect a piece of the Middle Ages: no words can tell you how its mingled beauty, history, and romance took hold on me; I can only say that, looking back on my past life, I find it was the greatest pleasure I have ever had: and now it is a pleasure which no one can ever have again: it is lost to the world for ever. At that time I was an undergraduate of Oxford. Though not so astounding, so romantic, or at first sight so mediaeval as the Norman city, Oxford in those days still kept a great deal of its earlier loveliness: and the memory of its grey streets as they then were has been an abiding influence and pleasure in my life, and would be greater still if I could only forget what they are now – a matter of far more importance than the so-called learning of the place could have been to me in any case, but which, as it was, no one tried to teach me, and I did not try to learn. Since then the guardians of this beauty and romance so fertile of education . . . are determined apparently to destroy it altogether. There is another pleasure for the world gone down the wind; here, again, the beauty and romance have been uselessly, causelessly, most foolishly thrown away. . . .

My work is the embodiment of dreams

Following his visit to France, Morris decided to become an architect. He became articled to G.E. Street (then architect to the Diocese of Oxford, and best known as the architect of the Law Courts, on the Strand, London). There Morris met Philip Webb, another life-long friend; after nine months spent copying the doorway of St Augustine's church in Canterbury ('the compass points nearly bored a hole through the drawing board', according to Webb), he abandoned architecture to become a painter, encouraged by Dante Gabriel Rossetti.

Morris began to write poetry as well as 'Romances' while he was at Oxford. 'Well if this is poetry it is very easy to write,' he is reported to have said when his friends acclaimed his efforts. He included some of these early poems in the Oxford and Cambridge Magazine *(including 'Riding Together'), but he had discarded most of them when he published* The Defence of Guenevere, and Other Poems *(at his own expense) in 1858. By the time the book was published, Morris (inspired by Rossetti) had abandoned architecture for painting, and he had also met and fallen in love with Jane Burden.*

WALTHAMSTOW, 6 OCT. 1855

To Cormell Price . . . I am going, if I can, to be an architect, and I am too old already and there is no time to lose, I MUST make haste, it would not do for me, dear Crom, even for the sake of being with you, to be a lazy, aimless, useless, dreaming body all my life long. I have wasted enough time already, God knows; not that I regret having gone to Oxford . . .

OXFORD, 11 NOV. 1855

To his mother I am almost afraid you thought me scarcely in earnest when I told you a month or two ago that I did not intend taking Holy Orders; if this is the case I am afraid also that my letter now may vex you; but if you have really made up your mind that I was in earnest I should hope you will be pleased with my resolution. You said then, you remember, and said very truly, that it was an evil thing to be an idle, objectless man; I am fully determined not to incur this reproach, I was so then though I did not tell you at the

25

APRIL LOVE, 1855

time all I thought of . . . partly because I had not thought about it enough myself, and partly because I wished to give you time to become reconciled to the idea of my continuing a lay person. I wish now to be an architect, an occupation I have often had hankering after, even during the time when I intended taking Holy Orders; the signs of wh: hankerings you yourself have doubtless often seen . . .

If I were not to follow this occupation I in truth know not what I should follow with any chance of success, or hope of happiness in my work, in this I am pretty confident I shall succeed, and make I hope a decent architect sooner or later; and you know too that in any work that one delights in, even the merest drudgery connected with it is delightful too – I shall be master too of a useful trade, one by wh: I should hope to earn money, not altogether precariously, if other things fail. . . it will be rather grievous to my pride and self-will to have to do just as I am told for three long years, but good for it too I think; rather grievous to any love of idleness and leisure to have to go through all the drudgery of learning a new trade, but for that also, good – Perhaps you think that people will laugh at me, and call me purposeless and changeable; I have no doubt they will, but I in my turn will try to shame them. God being my helper, by steadiness and hard work.

. . . I do not hope to be great at all in anything, but perhaps I may reasonably hope to be happy in my work, and sometimes when I am idle and doing nothing, pleasant visions go past me of the things that may be. . . .

OXFORD, 17 MAY 1856

To Edward Burne-Jones   . . . Will you do me a great favour, viz. go and nobble that picture called 'April Love' [by Arthur Hughes], as soon as possible lest anybody else should buy it . . .

OXFORD, JULY 1856

To Cormell Price   I have seen Rossetti twice since I saw the last of you; spent almost a whole day with him the last time, last Monday, that was. [H. Holman] Hunt came in while we were there, a tallish, slim man with a beautiful red beard, somewhat of a turn-up nose, and deep-set dark eyes: a beautiful man. . . . Rossetti says I ought to paint, he says I shall be able; now as he is a very great man, and speaks with authority and not as the scribes, I *must* try. I don't hope much, I must say, yet will try my best – he gave me practical advice on the subject. . . . So I am going to try, not giving up the architecture, but trying if it is possible to get six hours a day for drawing besides office work. One won't get much enjoyment out of life at this rate, I know well, but that don't matter: I have no right to ask for it at all events – love and work, these two things only. . . . I can't enter into politico-social subjects with any interest, for on the whole I see that things are in a muddle, and I have no power or vocation to set them right in ever so little a degree. My work is the embodiment of dreams in one form or another. . . .

From 'Frank's Sealed Letter'   . . . Ever since I can remember, even when I was quite a child, people have always told me that I had no perseverance, no strength of will; they have always kept on saying to me, directly and indirectly, 'Unstable as water, thou shall not excel'; and they have always been quite wrong in this matter, for of all men I have ever heard of, I have the strongest will for good and evil. I could soon find out whether a thing were possible or not to me; then if it were not, I threw it away for ever, never thought of it again, no regret, no longing for that, it was past and over to me; but if it were possible, and I made up my mind to do it, then and there I began it, and in due time finished it, turning neither to the right hand nor the left, till it was done. So I did with all things that I set my hand to. . . . Why! I never loved that woman there, with her heavy sweeping black hair, and dreamily passionate eyes; that was someone past away long ago. . . . I am the man that knows, that feels all poetry and art, that can create, that can sympathize with every man and woman that ever lived – even with that cold, proud woman there, without a heart, but with heavy, sweeping hair, and great dreamingly passionate eyes, which might cause a weak man to love her. . . .

From 'The Story of the Unknown Church'   . . . Then farther from the Church, and past the cloister and its buildings, were many detached buildings, and a great garden round them, all within the circle of the poplar trees; in the garden were trellises covered over with roses, and convolvolus, and the great-leaved fiery nasturtium; and specially all along by the poplar trees were there trellises, but on these grew nothing but deep crimson roses; the hollyhocks too were all out in blossom at that time, great spires of pink, and orange, and red, and white, with their soft, downy leaves. I said that nothing grew on the trellises by the poplars but crimson roses, but I was not quite right, for in many places the wild flowers had crept into the garden from without; lush green briony, with green-white blossoms, that grows so fast, one could almost think that we see it grow, and deadly nightshade, La bella donna, O! so beautiful; red berry, and purple, yellow-spiked flower, and deadly, cruel-looking, dark green leaf, all growing together in the glorious days of early autumn. . . .

From 'Svend and his Brethren'   . . . Siur stood in his own great hall (for his house was large), he stood before the daïs, and saw a fair sight, the work of his own hands.

For, fronting him, against the wall were seven thrones, and behind them a cloth of samite of purple wrought with golden stars, and barred across from right to left with long bars of silver and crimson, and edged below with melancholy, fading green, like a September sunset; and opposite each throne was a glittering suit of armour wrought wonderfully in bright steel, except that on the breast of each suit was a face worked marvellously in enamel, the face of Cissela in a glory of golden hair; and the glory of that gold spread away from the breast on all sides, and ran cunningly along with the steel rings, in such a way as it is hard even to imagine: moreover, on the crest of each helm was wrought the phoenix, the never-dying bird, the only creature that knows the sun; and by each suit lay a gleaming sword terrible to look at, steel from pommel to point, but wrought along the blade in burnished gold that outflashed the gleam of the steel, was written in fantastic letters the word 'Westward'. . . . .

From 'The Lindenborg Pool'   . . . Fierce as the wind was, it could not raise the leaden waters of that fearful pool, defended as they were by the steep banks of dripping yellow clay, striped horribly here and there with ghastly uncertain green and blue.

They said no man could fathom it; and yet all round the edges of it grew a rank crop of dreary reeds and segs, some round, some flat, but none ever flowering as other things flowered, never dying and being renewed, but always the same stiff array of unbroken reeds and segs, some round, some flat. Hard by me were two trees leafless and ugly, made, it seemed, only for the wind to go through with a wild sough on such nights as these; and for a mile from that place were no other trees. . . .

From The Defence of Guenevere and Other Poems

from 'Riding Together'

For many, many days together
   The wind blew steady from the East;
For many days hot grew the weather,
   About the time of our Lady's Feast.

For many days we rode together,
   Yet met we neither friend nor foe;
Hotter and clearer grew the weather,
   Steadily did the East wind blow.

We saw the trees in the hot, bright weather,
   Clear-cut, with shadows very black,
As freely we rode on together
   With helms unlaced and bridles slack.

And often, as we rode together,
   We, looking down the green-bank'd stream,
Saw flowers in the sunny weather,
   And saw the bubble-making bream.

And in the night lay down together,
   And hung above our heads the rood,
Or watch'd night-long in the dewy weather,
   The while the moon did watch the wood.

Our spears stood bright and thick together,
   Straight out the banners stream'd behind,
As we gallop'd on in the sunny weather,
   With faces turn'd towards the wind.

from 'The Defence of Guenevere'

'. . . From out my memory; I hear thrushes sing,
And wheresoever I may be, straightway
Thoughts of it all come up with most fresh sting;

'I was half mad with beauty on that day,
And went without my ladies all alone,
In a quiet garden walled round every way;

'I was right joyful of that wall of stone,
That shut the flowers and trees up with the sky,
And trebled all the beauty: . . .

'. . . But shortly listen – In that garden fair

'Came Launcelot walking; this is true, the kiss
Wherewith we kissed in meeting that spring day,
I scarce dare talk of the remember'd bliss,

'When both our mouths went wandering in one way,
And aching sorely, met among the leaves;
Our hands being left behind strained far away.

'Never within a yard of my bright sleeves
Had Launcelot come before – and now, so nigh!
After that day why is it Guenevere grieves? . . .'

from 'Sir Peter Harpdon's End'

. . . Edward the prince lies underneath the ground,
Edward the king is dead, at Westminster
The carvers smooth the curls of his long beard,
Everything goes to rack – eh! and we too.
Now, Curzon, listen; if they come, these French,
Whom have I got to lean on here, but you?
A man can die but once, will you die then,
Your brave sword in your hand, thoughts in your heart
Of all the deeds we have done here in France –
And yet may do? So God will have your soul,
Whoever has your body.

from 'The Haystack in the Floods'

Had she come all the way for this,
To part at last without a kiss?
Yea, had she borne the dirt and rain
That her own eyes might see him slain
Beside the haystack in the floods?

Along the dripping leafless woods,
The stirrup touching either shoe,
She rode astride as troopers do;
With kirtle kilted to her knee,
To which the mud splash'd wretchedly;
And the wet dripp'd from every tree
Upon her head and heavy hair,
And on her eyelids broad and fair;
The tears and rain ran down her face.

By fits and starts they rode apace,
And very often was his place
Far off from her; he had to ride
Ahead, to see what might betide
When the roads cross'd; and sometimes, when
There rose a murmuring from his men,
Had to turn back with promises;
Ah me! she had but little ease;
And often for pure doubt and dread
She sobb'd, made giddy in the head
By the swift riding; while, for cold,

Her slender fingers scarce could hold
The wet reins: yea, and scarcely, too,
She felt the foot within her shoe
Against the stirrup: all for this,
To part at last without a kiss
Beside the haystack in the floods. . . .

from 'Golden Wings'

Midways of a walled garden,
     In the happy poplar land,
     Did an ancient castle stand,
With an old knight for a warden.

Many scarlet bricks there were
     In its walls, and old grey stone;
     Over which red apples shone
At the right time of the year.

On the bricks the green moss grew,
     Yellow lichen on the stone,
     Over which red apples shone;
Little war that castle knew.

Deep green water fill'd the moat,
     Each side had a red-brick lip,
     Green and mossy with the drip
Of dew and rain; there was a boat

Of carven wood, with hangings green
     About the stern; it was great bliss
     For lovers to sit there and kiss
In the hot summer noons, not seen. . . .

'Summer Dawn'

Pray but one prayer for me 'twixt thy closed lips,
Think but one thought of me up in the stars.
The summer night waneth, the morning light slips,
Faint and grey 'twixt the leaves of the aspen, betwixt the
     cloud bars,
That are patiently waiting there for the dawn:
Patient and colourless, though Heaven's gold
Waits to float through them along with the sun.
Far out in the meadows, above the young corn,
The heavy elms wait, and restless and cold
The uneasy wind rises; the roses are dun;
Through the long twilight they pray for the dawn,
Round the lone house in the midst of the corn.
Speak but one word to me over the corn,
Over the tender, bow'd locks of the corn.

from 'The Eve of Crecy'

Gold on her head, and gold on her feet,
And gold where the hems of her kirtle meet,
And a golden girdle round my sweet; —
   Ah! qu'elle est belle La Marguerite.

Margaret's maids are fair to see,
Freshly dressed and pleasantly;
Margaret's hair falls down to her knee;
   Ah! qu'elle est belle La Marguerite.

If I were rich I would kiss her feet,
I would kiss the place where the gold hems meet,
And the golden girdle round my sweet —
   Ah! qu'elle est belle La Marguerite. . . .

'In Prison'

Wearily, drearily,
Half the day long,
Flap the great banners
High over the stone;
Strangely and eerily
Sounds the wind's song,
Bending the banner poles.

While, all alone,
Watching the loophole's spark,
Lie I, with life all dark,
Feet tether'd, hands fetter'd
Fast to the stone,
The grim walls, square letter'd
With prison'd men's groan.

Still strain the banner-poles
Through the wind's song,
Westward the banner rolls
Over my wrong.

Work and love

In the autumn of 1856, G.E. Street moved his office to London, and Morris came with him. He shared a room with Edward Burne-Jones in Bloomsbury, and they both went to life drawing classes in the evenings: 'Topsy and I live together in the quaintest room in all London,' wrote Edward Burne-Jones, 'hung with brasses of old knights and drawings of Albert Dürer. We know Rossetti now as a daily friend, and we know Browning too, who is the greatest poet alive. . . . Topsy will be a painter, he works hard, is prepared to wait twenty years, loves art more and more every day . . .'

Morris finally abandoned his architectural apprenticeship early in 1857 in order to concentrate on painting, and it was then that he and Ned moved into rooms in Red Lion Square. The rooms were unfurnished, so they designed their own furniture — a table, a chair and a settle.

In the summer of 1857 Rossetti was commissioned to supervise the decoration of the ceiling of the debating hall in the new Oxford Union Building, designed by Benjamin Woodward. He enlisted his friends, none of them experienced in mural painting, and they set to work with enthusiasm. Inevitably, the work began to deteriorate, and Morris redecorated the roof in 1875.

He wrote a brief account of the venture in 1869 in a letter to James Thursfield. The stay in Oxford was an important time for Morris, for this is when he met his future wife, Jane Burden.

'If we needed models, we sat to each other, and Morris had a head always fit for Launcelot or Tristram,' said Edward Burne-Jones. 'For the purposes of our drawing we needed armour, and of a date and design so remote that no examples existed for our use. Therefore Morris, whose knowledge of these things seemed to have been born in him, and who never at any time needed books of reference for anything, set to work to make designs for an ancient kind of helmet called a basinet, and for a great surcoat of ringed mail with a hood of mail and the skirt coming below the knees. They were made for him by a stout little smith who had a forge near the Castle. Morris's visits to the forge were daily, but what scenes happened there we shall never know; the encounters between these two workmen were always stubborn and angry as far as I could see. One afternoon when I was working high up at my picture, I heard a strange bellowing in the building, and turning round to find the cause, saw an unwonted sight. The basinet was being tried on, but the visor, for some reason, would not lift, and I saw Morris embedded in iron, dancing with rage and roaring inside. The mail coat came in due time, and was so satisfactory to its designer that the first day it came he chose to dine in it. It became him well; he looked very splendid. When it lay in coils on the ground, one could lift it with great difficulty, but once put on the body its weight was so evenly ordered that it was less uncomfortable than any top coat I ever wore.'

JANE BURDEN, 1857

WILLIAM MORRIS PRESENTING A RING TO JANE BURDEN, 1857

from 'Praise of My Lady'

My lady seems of ivory
Forehead, straight nose, and cheeks that be
Hollow'd a little mournfully.
　　　　Beata mea Domina!

Her forehead, overshadow'd much
By bows of hair, has a wave such
As God was good to make for me.
　　　　Beata mea Domina!

Nor greatly long my lady's hair,
Nor yet with yellow colour fair,
But thick and crisped wonderfully:
　　　　Beata mea Domina!

Heavy to make the pale face sad,
And dark, but dead as though it had
Been forged by God most wonderfully
　　　　—Beata mea Domina!—

Of some strange metal, thread by thread,
To stand out from my lady's head,
Not moving much to tangle me.
　　　　Beata mea Domina!

Beneath her brows the lids fall slow,
The lashes a clear shadow throw
Where I would wish my lips to be.
　　　　Beata mea Domina!

Her great eyes, standing far apart,
Draw up some memory from her heart,
And gaze out very mournfully;
　　　　—Beata mea Domina!—

So beautiful and kind they are,
But most times looking out afar,
Waiting for something, not for me.
　　　　—Beata mea Domina!—

To James Thursfield   I am sorry you are in trouble about the works at the Union, and hope I shan't increase it by my letter: I can speak distinctly about two of the pictures in question, Mr. Hughes', the one at the North End, and Mr. Burne-Jones' (Nimue and Merlin). Of these I think the design of Mr. Hughes to be quite among the best works of that painter, and a very beautiful and remarkable one: I think I have been told it is in a bad state, but I suppose something might be done to it. Mr. Burne-Jones' is a beautiful work, and admirably suits its space as to decoration; it would be quite absurd to cover it up. Mr. Pollen's, opposite Mr. Hughes' was never finished; two others, one by Mr. Prinsep, another by Mr. Stanhope, though not very complete in some ways, yet looked very well in their places I think. As for my own, I believe it *has* some merits as to colour, but I must confess I should feel much more comfortable if it had disappeared from the wall, as I am conscious of its being extremely ludicrous in many ways. In confidence to you I should say that the whole affair was begun and carried out in too piecemeal and unorganised a manner to be a real success – nevertheless it would surely be a pity to destroy some of the pictures, which are really remarkable, and at the worst can do no harm there. . . .

THE OXFORD UNION MURALS,
1857

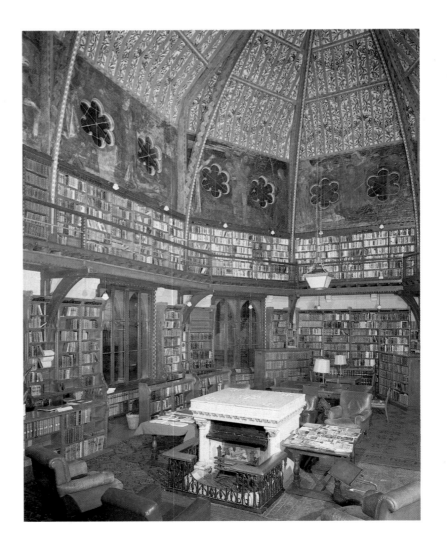

FINE ART WORKMEN

Red House, Philip Webb's first commission, was completed for the Morrises in the summer of 1860 and William and Janey moved in, keeping open house for their friends. Burne-Jones and Georgiana Macdonald were married that June, and Rossetti had married Lizzie Siddall. They were frequent visitors, as were the painters involved in the Oxford Union project:

'O the joy of those Saturdays to Mondays at Red House!' wrote one of these visitors (quoted in Mackail), 'the getting out at Abbey Wood Station and smelling the sweet air, and then the scrambling, swinging drive of three miles or so to the house; and the beautiful roomy place where we seemed to be coming home just as much as when we returned to our own rooms.' 'It was the most beautiful sight in the world,' according to another, 'to see Morris coming up from the cellar before dinner, beaming with joy,

RED HOUSE, BEXLEYHEATH, KENT, 1860

UPPER LANDING, RED HOUSE

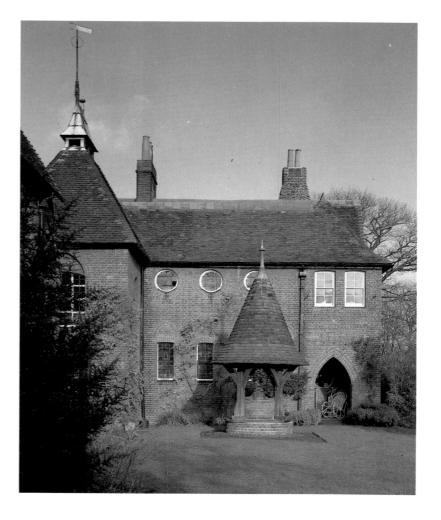

with his hands full of bottles of wine and others tucked under his arms.'

The Morrises' two children were born there – Jenny (Jane Alice) in January 1861, and May (Mary) in March the following year. Soon after they moved in, however, Morris and his friends got down to decorating and furnishing it. It was this enterprise that led to the formation of the Firm.

Morris, Marshall, Faulkner and Co., Fine Art Workmen in Painting, Carving, Furniture and the Metals, was launched in April 1861. As well as Webb, and the Oxford Brotherhood trio (Morris, Faulkner and Burne-Jones), the founder members included Rossetti, the painter Ford Madox Brown, and Peter Paul Marshall, who was a friend of Madox Brown's. (Arthur Hughes, co-opted in his absence, declined to join . . . he lived 'in the country' and said he would find it difficult to get to the meetings.)

Workshops were set up in 8 Red Lion Square, near to the former lodgings of Morris and Burne-Jones. The first floor was an office and a showroom, and the third floor and the basement

RED HOUSE INTERIORS

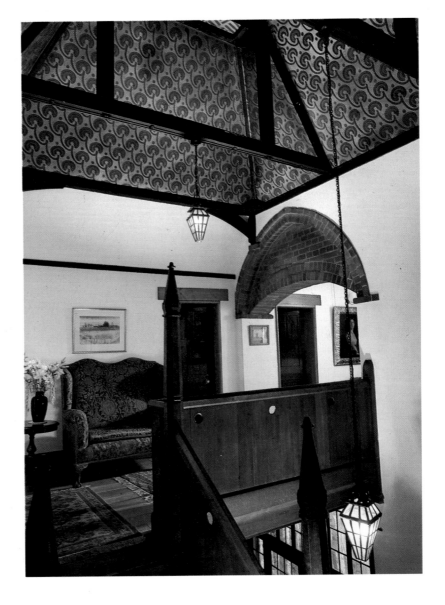

were used as workshops (with a small kiln in the basement). 'As the work grew on their hands,' wrote Mackail, 'about a dozen men and boys came to be regularly employed on the premises. The boys were got from a Boys' Home in the Euston Road; the men chiefly from Camden Town. The foreman, Mr George Campfield, was a glass-painter who had come under Morris's notice as a pupil in the evening classes of the Working Men's College in Great Ormond Street.'

Morris was finding it difficult to 'commute' between Red House and Red Lion Square. At first the plan was to move the workshops to the house, and to build another wing for Ned and Georgiana. In the summer of 1864, however, the Burne-Joneses fell ill with scarlet fever ... Georgiana was desperately ill, and their three-week-old son died. Burne-Jones, who needed every penny he could get from painting as well as stained glass commissions, decided to stay in London, and Morris, reluctantly, had to give up Red House. He never went back there.

RED HOUSE, 18 JAN. 1861

To Ford Madox Brown   Kid having appeared, Mrs Brown kindly says she will stay till Monday, when you are to come to fetch her, please. I send a list of trains in evening to Abbey Wood met by bus, viz., from London Bridge, 2.20 p.m., 4.20 p.m., 6.0 p.m., and 7.15 p.m. Janey and kid (girl) are both very well.

From a circular advertising the Firm   MORRIS, MARSHALL, FAULKNER & CO., FINE ART WORKMEN IN PAINTING, CARVING, FURNITURE, AND THE METALS

FORD MADOX BROWN	ARTHUR HUGHES	D. G. ROSSETTI
EDWARD BURNE-JONES	P. P. MARSHALL	PHILIP WEBB
C. J. FAULKNER	WILLIAM MORRIS	

The growth of Decorative Art in this country, owing to the efforts of English Architects, has now reached a point at which it seems desirable that Artists of reputation should devote their time to it. Although no doubt particular instances of success may be cited, still it must be generally felt that attempts of this kind hitherto have been crude and fragmentary. Up to this time, the want of that artistic supervision, which can alone bring about harmony between the various parts of a successful work, has been increased by the necessarily excessive outlay, consequent on taking one individual artist from his pictorial labours.

The Artists whose names appear above hope by association to do away with this difficulty. Having among their number men of varied qualifications, they will be able to undertake any species of decoration, mural or otherwise, from pictures, properly so-called, down to the consideration of the smallest work susceptible of art beauty. It is anticipated that by such co-operation, the largest amount of what is essentially the artist's work, along with his constant supervision, will be secured at the smallest possible expense, while the work done must necessarily be of a much more complete order, than if any single artist were incidentally employed in the usual manner.

These Artists having for many years been deeply attached to the study of the Decorative Arts of all times and countries, have felt more than most people the want of some one place, where they could either obtain or get produced work of a genuine and beautiful character.

PAGES FROM WILLIAM MORRIS'S SKETCHBOOKS,
DATE UNKNOWN

They have therefore now established themselves as a firm, for the production, by themselves and under their supervision, of—

I. Mural Decoration, either in Pictures or in Pattern Work, or merely in the arrangement of Colours, as applied to dwelling-houses, churches, or public buildings.

II. Carving generally, as applied to Architecture.

III. Stained Glass, especially with reference to its harmony with Mural Decoration.

IV. Metal Work in all its branches, including Jewellery.

V. Furniture, either depending for its beauty on its own design, on the application of materials hitherto overlooked, or on its conjunction with Figure and Pattern Painting. Under this head is included Embroidery of all kinds, stamped leather, and ornamental work in other such materials, besides every article necessary for domestic use.

It is only requisite to state further, that all work of all the above classes will be estimated for, and executed in a businesslike manner; and it is believed that good decoration, involving rather the luxury of taste than the luxury of costliness, will be found to be much less expensive than is generally supposed.

RED LION SQUARE, 19 APRIL 1861

To Frederick Barlow Guy   By reading the enclosed you will see that I have started as a decorator which I have long meant to do when I could get men of reputation to join me, and to this end mainly I have built my fine house. You see we are, or consider ourselves to be, the only really artistic firm of the kind, the others being only glass painters in point of fact, (like Clayton & Bell) or else that curious nondescript mixture of clerical tailor and decorator that flourishes in Southampton Street, Strand; whereas we shall do – most things. However, what we are most anxious to get at present is wall-decoration, and I want to know if you could be so kind as to send me (without troubling yourself) a list of clergymen and others, to whom it *might* be any use to send a circular. In about a month we shall have some things to show in these rooms, painted cabinets, embroidery and all the rest of it, and perhaps you could look us up then: I suppose till the holidays you couldn't come down to Red House: I was very much disappointed that you called when I was out before.

RED HOUSE, NOV. 1864

To Edward Burne-Jones   As to our palace of Art, I confess your letter was a blow to me at first, though hardly an unexpected one – in short I cried; but I have got over it now. As to our being a miserable lot, old chap, speaking for myself I don't know, I refuse to make myself really unhappy for any thing short of the loss of friends one can't do without. Suppose in all these troubles you had given us the slip what the devil should I have done? I am sure I couldn't have had the heart to have gone on with the firm: all our jolly subjects would have gone to pot – it frightens me to think of, Ned. But now I am only 30 years old, I shan't always have the rheumatism, and we shall have a lot of jolly years of invention and lustre plates together I hope. I need hardly tell you how I suffered for you in the worst of your troubles; on the Saturday I had begun a letter to you but it read so dismal (as indeed I felt little hope) that I burnt it. . . .

QUEEN SQUARE

Living above the shop

Morris and his family moved into 26 Queen Square, Bloomsbury, in 1865. The ground floor was turned into an office and showroom, and a large ballroom became the main workshop. Other workshops were established in a courtyard at the back, and in the adjacent Ormond Yard.

Living on the premises, Morris took control of the workshop production. Charles Faulkner, a mathematician rather than a business manager, decided to return to Oxford, and Warington Taylor, an old Etonian who had fallen on hard times, took over from Faulkner in 1865. Taylor took his new responsibilities very seriously. He was infuriated by what he described as the partners' 'unprofessional behaviour' and 'general British muddle', urging 'accuracy and method', qualities he found singularly lacking in 'the guvnor'. Taylor had tuberculosis, and spent a great deal of his time in Hastings, bombarding the partners (especially Webb and Rossetti) with letters. Significantly, he seemed to be the only member of the Firm at that time to demonstrate a social conscience: 'Just remember we are embezzling public money now,' he wrote of the prestigious commission to decorate the Armoury and Tapestry Room at St James's Palace; 'what business has any palace to be decorated at all?' Again, he complained of the cost (and the impracticality) of the Firm's furniture: 'It is hellish wickedness to spend 15/- on a chair when the poor are starving in the street'; what was needed, he said, was something light and inexpensive – qualities which he found in the so-called 'Sussex' rush-seated chairs, variants of which continued to be produced by the Firm after Morris's death. He also wrote to Webb suggesting the introduction of the adjustable chair, enclosing a sketch of 'a chair model of which I saw with an old carpenter at Hurstmonceaux, Sussex, by name Ephraim Coleman – back and seat made with bars across to put a cushion on – moving on a hinge.'

During this period, however, the Firm was establishing its reputation with several important commissions. The architect G.F. Bodley was their first patron, commissioning stained glass and decorative schemes for St Michael's, Brighton, All Saints, Selsley, and Jesus College Chapel, Cambridge, in the early 1860s. The St James's Palace commission came at the end of 1866, and the Firm was asked to design the Green Dining Room at the South Kensington Museum (now known as the Victoria & Albert Museum) in 1867.

QUEEN SQUARE, LATE JUNE 1866

To Frederick R. Leach   I am informed by Mr. Bodley for whom you have done some work that you would probably undertake the execution of certain decorations we are about to commence in Jesus Chapel. The work is to be in distemper to be done in the best & most workmanlike manner to be finished to the approval both as to colour and execution.

We shall begin on the ceiling of the tower. I shall be coming down to Cambridge with Mr Bodley on Thursday 5 July & should wish you by that time to have whitened sufficiently the tower ceiling for a ground. The white should have no blueblack mixed with it. If you could also manage it I should wish you to paint in at least one of the enclosed pattern on the smaller panels. This pattern must be placed so that the J H C can be read from the ground by one looking East.

I send with this patterns of colour for the flowers & leaves which I should wish to be closely followed. I shall be obliged by an answer by return as to whether you can do this & will then tell you by what train Mr. Bodley & I will come next Thursday.

QUEEN SQUARE, 22 MARCH 1867

To George Campfield   We send money £5. I think I shall be coming on Monday [to Jesus College], but if any of the fellows ask when, say you don't know; you must manage to finish next week. . . . The escapades of our men have enraged the dons and they want to get rid of you. I send the two last cartoons and with them a cartoon of an angel piping for the triangular space below the crossing arch. You must draw the wings (gold) yourself . . .

QUEEN SQUARE, 14 DEC. 1868

To Frederick R. Leach   We send you the drawings & specification of the two screens [for St Mary's Church, Beddington, Surrey] – The drawings are traced from the first designs & are not quite accurate . . .

You will provide for painting the *doors* of the chancel screen *first* so as to be able [to] send them to us *here* as soon as may be – We shall paint all the panels – but no more – Can you lay

GREEN DINING ROOM AT THE SOUTH KENSINGTON MUSEUM, 1867

or get laid a proper painting ground on the panels of the chancel screen? It would be desirable to have this done before the mouldings are painted . . .

Tell us if you find any great differences between the drawings & the finished work –

In making your estimate you may consider that the pattern work will be simple & not very profuse but you had better err in excess than defect

We shall be glad to have your estimate as soon as you can make it –

Please return the drawings

The Earthly Paradise

Following the private publication of The Defence of Guenevere *in 1858, Morris did not involve himself with publishing again until 1867, when* The Life and Death of Jason *appeared, to popular acclaim. The success of* Jason *was encouraging, because it was part of a major project (Morris called it the 'Big Book') which he had been planning, writing, and reading to his friends throughout the 1860s.*

The Earthly Paradise, *which established Morris's reputation as a poet, was published in three volumes – the first in 1868, and the second two in 1870 (*Jason *was to have been part of it, but it proved to be so long that Morris decided to publish it separately).* The Earthly Paradise *was conceived as an epic poem, in the manner of Chaucer. It describes how 'Certain gentlemen and mariners of Norway, having considered all that they had heard of the Earthly Paradise, set sail to find it, and after many troubles, and the lapse of many years came old men to some Western Land, of which they had never before heard; there they died, when they had dwelt there certain years, much honoured of the strange people.'*

As the 'Wanderers' travel, they tell stories to their hosts, who return the compliment: there are two stories for each month of the year, and each month is introduced by its own poem. The epic begins in March, in spring time, with the invocation:

> *Forget six counties overhung with smoke,*
> *Forget the snorting steam and piston stroke,*
> *Forget the spreading of the hideous town;*
> *Think rather of the pack-horse on the down,*
> *And dream of London, small, and white, and clean,*
> *The clear Thames bordered by its gardens green; . . .*

Throughout the 1860s, however, as Morris continued to write, his youthful optimism diminished; the loss of Red House and its promise of continuity and a family life was a real blow to him, but now he was losing his wife. Woven into the narrative of the poetry there is what Mackail described as 'an autobiography so outspoken that it needs to be left to speak for itself'. The 'autobiography' is most evident in the poems introducing each month, which become bleaker as the year progresses; 'The Hill of Venus', which completes the epic, contains some of the most despairing of the poetry.

PHOTOGRAPH OF JANE MORRIS, 1865

From The Life and Death of Jason

'And now behold within the haven rides
Our good ship, swinging in the changing tides,
Gleaming with gold, and blue, and cinnabar,
The long new oars beside the rowlocks are,
The sail hangs flapping in the light west wind,
Nor aught undone can any craftsman find
From stem to stern; so is our quest begun
To-morrow at the rising of the sun.
And may Jove bring us all safe back to see
Another sun shine on this fair city,
When elders and the flower-crowned maidens meet
With tears and singing our returning feet.'

*

Their longing eyes beheld a lovely land,
Green meadows rising o'er a yellow strand,
Well-set with fair fruit-bearing trees, and groves
Of thick-leaved elms all populous of doves,

And watered by a wandering clear green stream
And through the trees they saw a palace gleam
Of polished marble, fair beyond man's thought.
    There as they lay, the sweetest scents were brought
By sighing winds across the bitter sea,
And languid music breathed melodiously,
Steeping their souls in such unmixed delight,
That all their hearts grew soft, and dim of sight
They grew, and scarce their hands could grip the oar,
And as they slowly neared the happy shore
The young men well-nigh wept, and e'en the wise
Thought they had reached the gate of Paradise.

From The Earthly Paradise

Dreamer of dreams, born out of my due time,
Why should I strive to set the crooked straight?
Let it suffice me that my murmuring rhyme
Beats with light wing against the ivory gate,
Telling a tale not too importunate
To those who in the sleepy region stay,
Lulled by the singer of an empty day.

Folk say, a wizard to a northern king
At Christmas-tide such wondrous things did show,
That through one window men beheld the spring,
And through another saw the summer glow,
And through a third the fruited-vines a-row,
While still, unheard, but in its wonted way,
Piped the drear wind of that December day.

So with this Earthly Paradise it is,
If ye will read aright, and pardon me,
Who strive to build a shadowy isle of bliss
Midmost the beating of the steely sea,
Where tossed about all hearts of men must be;
Whose ravening monsters mighty men shall slay,
Not the idle singer of an empty day.

from 'Ogier the Dane'

Haec
In the white-flowered hawthorn-brake,
Love, be merry for my sake;
Twine the blossoms in my hair,
Kiss me where I am most fair —
Kiss me, love! for who knoweth
What thing cometh after death?

Ille
Nay, the garlanded gold hair
Hides thee where thou art most fair;
Hides the rose-tipped hills of snow —
Ah! sweet love, I have thee now!
Kiss me love! for who knoweth
What thing cometh after death?

from 'The Son of Croesus'

They left the house, and, following up the stream,
In the low sun saw the kingfisher gleam
'Twixt bank and alder, and the grebe steal out
From the high sedge, and, in his restless doubt,
Dive down, and rise to see what men were there;
They saw the swallow chase high up in air
The circling gnats; the shaded dusky pool
Broke by the splashing chub; the ripple cool,
Rising and falling, of some distant weir
They heard, till it oppressed the listening ear,
As twilight grew; so back they turned again
Glad of their rest, and pleasure after pain.

from 'The Story of Cupid and Psyche'

But when a little Psyche's eyes grew clear,
A sight they saw that brought back all her fear
A hundred-fold, though neither heaven nor earth
To such a fair sight elsewhere could give birth;
Because apart, upon a golden throne
Of marvellous work, a woman sat alone,
Watching the dancers with a smiling face,
Whose beauty sole had lighted up the place.
A crown there was upon her glorious head,
A garland round about her girdlestead,
Where matchless wonders of the hidden sea
Were brought together and set wonderfully,
Naked she was of all else, but her hair
About her body rippled here and there,
And lay in heaps upon the golden seat,
And even touched the gold cloth where her feet
Lay amid roses — ah, how kind she seemed!
What depths of love from out her grey eyes beamed!

from 'The Hill of Venus'

How can words measure misery when the sun
Shines at its brightest over plague and ill?
How can I tell the woe of any-one,
When the soft showers with fair-hued sweetness fill
Before the feet of those grief may not kill,
The tender meads of hopeful spring, that comes
With eager hours to mock all hopeless homes?

So let it pass, and ask me not to weigh
Grief against grief; – ye who have ever woke
To wondering, ere came memory back, why day,
Bare, blank, immovable upon you broke –
– Untold shall ye know all – to happy folk
All heaviest words no more meaning bear
Than far off bells saddening the summer air. . . .

Time and again, he, listening to such word,
Felt his heart kindle; time and again did seem
As though a cold and hopeless tune he heard,
Sung by grey mouths amidst a dull-eyed dream;
Time and again across his heart would stream
The pain of fierce desire whose aim was gone,
Of baffled yearning, loveless and alone.

from 'Pygmalion and the Image'

Thus to his chamber at the last he came,
And, pushing through the still half-opened door,
He stood within; but there, for very shame
Of all the things that he had done before,
Still kept his eyes bent down upon the floor,
Thinking of all that he had done and said
Since he had wrought that luckless marble maid.

Yet soft his thoughts were, and the very place
Seemed perfumed with some nameless heavenly air;
So gaining courage, did he raise his face
Unto the work his hands had made so fair,
And cried aloud to see the niche all bare
Of that sweet form, while through his heart again
There shot a pang of his old yearning pain.

Yet while he stood, and knew not what to do,
With yearning a strange thrill of hope there came:
A shaft of new desire now pierced him through,
And therewithal a soft voice called his name,
And when he turned, with eager eyes aflame,
He saw betwixt him and the setting sun
The lively image of his loved one.

JANE MORRIS, 1869

from 'September'

Look long, O longing eyes, and look in vain!
Strain idly, aching heart, and yet be wise,
And hope no more for things to come again
That thou beheldest once with careless eyes!
Like a new-wakened man thou art, who tries
To dream again the dream that made him glad
When in his arms his loving love he had.

WILLIAM MORRIS WITH JENNY AND MAY MORRIS, *c.* 1865

'November'

Are thine eyes weary? is thy heart too sick
To struggle any more with doubt and thought,
Whose formless veil draws darkening now and thick
Across thee, e'en as smoke-tinged mist-wreaths brought
Down a fair dale to make it blind and nought?
Art thou so weary that no world there seems
Beyond these four walls, hung with pain and dreams?

Look out upon the real world, where the moon,
Half-way 'twixt root and crown of these high trees,
Turns the dead midnight into dreamy noon,
Silent and full of wonders, for the breeze
Died at the sunset, and no images,
No hopes of day, are left in sky or earth—
Is it not fair, and of most wondrous worth?

Yea, I have looked, and seen November there;
The changeless seal of change it seemed to be.
Fair death of things that, living once, were fair;
Bright sign of loneliness too great for me,
Strange image of the dread eternity,
In whose void patience how can these have part,
These outstretched feverish hands, this restless heart?

'January'

From this dull rainy undersky and low,
This murky ending of a leaden day,
That never knew the sun, this half-thawed snow,
These tossing black boughs faint against the grey
Of gathering night, thou turnest, dear, away
Silent, but with thy scarce-seen kindly smile
Sent through the dusk my longing to beguile.

There, the lights gleam, and all is dark without!
And in the sudden change our eyes meet dazed—
O look, love, look again! the veil of doubt
Just for one flash, past counting, then was raised!
O eyes of heaven, as clear thy sweet soul blazed
On mine a moment! O come back again
Strange rest and dear amid the long dull pain!

Nay, nay, gone by! though there she sitteth still,
With wide grey eyes so frank and fathomless—
Be patient, heart, thy days they yet shall fill
With utter rest—Yea, now thy pain they bless,
And feed thy last hope of the world's redress—
O unseen hurrying rack! O wailing wind!
What rest and where go ye this night to find?

A cold and hopeless tune

During the late 1860s and early 1870s Morris used poetry as a means of expressing his personal despair, and the autobiography that was so evident in the later poems of The Earthly Paradise *was even more explicit in other poems written at this period that were not published in his lifetime. In these, Janey's withdrawal and Morris's sense of isolation are clearly expressed. The emotional strain obviously began to affect Janey's health, and in the summer of 1869 Morris took her to a German spa – an experience which, judging from Morris's letters to Philip Webb, neither of them enjoyed, although Morris used the time to continue writing* The Earthly Paradise. *Persuading himself that Janey's health had improved, Morris returned to a new enthusiasm; he had 'discovered' Icelandic sagas when he was writing 'The Lovers of Gudrun' for* The Earthly Paradise *and he began, with the help of Eiríkr Magnússon to read and translate from the Icelandic. He also paid tribute to Georgiana Burne-Jones, who had her own sorrows, in the exquisite* Book of Verse *which he wrote and 'illuminated' as a present for her.*

WILLIAM MORRIS, PORTRAIT BY G.F. WATTS, 1870

from 'Near But Far Away'

She wavered, stopped and turned, methought her eyes,
    The deep grey windows of her heart, were wet,
    Methought they softened with a near regret
To note in mine unspoken miseries:
And as a prayer from out my heart did rise
    And struggle on my lips in shame's strong net,
    She stayed me, and cried 'Brother!' Our lips met.
Her hands drew me into Paradise.
Sweet seemed that kiss till thence her feet were gone,
    Sweet seemed the word she spake, while it might be
    As wordless music – But truth fell on me
And kiss and word I knew, and, left alone,
Face to face seemed I to a wall of stone,
While at my back there beat a boundless sea. . . .

'MORRIS READING POETRY TO BURNE-JONES'

'Why Dost Thou Struggle'

Why dost thou struggle, strive for victory
Over my heart that loveth thine so well?
When Death shall one day have its will of thee
And to deaf ears thy triumph thou must tell.

Unto deaf ears or unto such as know
The hearts of dead and living wilt thou say:
'A childish heart there loved me once and lo
I took his love and cast his love away.

'A childish greedy heart! yet still he clung
So close to me that much he pleased my pride
And soothed a sorrow that about me hung
With glimpses of his love unsatisfied . . .

'But now my heart grown silent of its grief
Saw more than kindness in his hungry eyes
But I must wear a mask of false belief
And feign that nought I know his miseries.

'I wore a mask because though certainly
I loved him not yet was there something soft
And sweet to have him ever loving me
Belike it is I well nigh loved him oft—

'Nigh loved him oft and needs must grant to him
Some kindness out of all he asked of me
And hoped his love would still hang vague, dim,
About my life like half-heard melody.

'He knew my heart and over-well knew this
And strove poor soul to pleasure me herein;
But yet what might he do? some doubtful kiss,
Some word, some look might give him hope to win.

'Poor hope, poor soul, for he again would come
Thinking to gain yet one more golden step
Toward love's shrine and lo! the kind speech dumb
The kind look gone, no love upon my lip—

'Yea gone, yet not my fault. I knew of love,
But my love and not his; nor could I tell
That such blind passion in him I should move.
Behold, I have loved faithfully and well!'

'Love of my love so deep and measureless
O Lords of the new world this too ye know
                                    (unfinished)

'Guileful Love'

Love set me in a flowery garden fair
Love showed me many marvels flowering there
Love said Take these, if nought thy soul doth dare
To feel my fiery hand upon thine heart,
Take these, and live, and lose the better part.

Love showed me Death, and said Make no delay
Love showed me Change, and said, Joy ebbs away
Love showed me Eld amid regrets grown grey
I laughed for joy, and round his heart I clung,
Sickened and swooned by bitter sweetness stung

But I awoke at last, and born again
Laid eager hands upon unrest and pain
And wrapped myself about with longing vain
Ah, better still and better all things grew
As more the root and heart of Love I knew

O Love Love Love, what is it thou has done?
All pains, all fears I knew, save only one;
Where is the fair earth now, where is the sun?
Thou didst not say my Love might never move
Her eyes, her hands, her lips to bless my love.

'THE M'S AT EMS', 1869

'Song'

Hearken: nigher still and nigher
Had we grown, methought my fire
Woke in her some hidden flame
And the rags of pride and shame
She seemed casting from her heart,
And the dull days seemed to part;
Then I cried out, 'Ah I move thee
And thou knowest that I love thee.'
Half-forgotten, unforgiven and alone!
Alone, unhappy by the fire I sat . . .

We meet we laugh and talk, but still is set
A seal over things I never can forget
But must not speak of still. I count the hours
That bring my friend to me – with hungry eyes
I watch him as his feet the staircase mount.
Then face to face we sit, a wall of lies
Made hard by fear and faint anxieties
Is drawn between us and he goes away
And leaves me wishing it were yesterday.

To Philip Webb   That is really my address though it looks like chaff, and I am not like to move now during the time of our captivity; I am so jolly glad to have got over the journey on no worse terms, once or twice I felt quite enclined to give in, but here we are and Janey is certainly no worse than when we started. . . . J has seen the Dr. twice and has had 4 baths and a corresponding amount of luke-warm Spa-water which she drinks in the morning before breakfast; I took her a drive of about 5 miles and back on Thursday; she seemed better for it the next day; 2 other days I paddled her about the river in a machine like a butter-boat with a knife and fork for oars; this they call a gondola here . . . there is a nice green bank in shadow after 5 P.M. just this side of the rapids, and I suppose I shall paddle Janey there pretty often; till she gets better it is like to be her principal enjoyment as the carriage business shakes her too much; if ('when' I hope) she gets better there are splendid mokes and mules here, whereon she may climb the hills . . .

 . . . The last few days while Janey has been queer & bilious we have found it rather hard to get such grub as she could comfortably eat, however I have arranged that now; she gets on pretty well with the drink, and we both like the beer here; it is easier to digest I think than English beer, and doesn't make one sleepy . . .

 . . . The weather has quite broken down today is a regular wet day and O lord can't it rain at Ems – I went a two hours walk yesterday up a hill-road; I think the country very jolly I must say; it all runs towards the big gorge in little gorges, the centres of which are all grass and hold the moisture like a cup and are as green as green can be, one little valley I came to was so jolly; a flat green space with alders round two sides of it, the great hills in the distance at one end and round the other the hills rising steep with great lanky beech woods – as dry as a bone – There is nothing of the common-place about the ordinary nature here, it is a wonderful country and fit for the breeding of German sentiment – I have been reading Carlyle's Wilhelm Meister and have got through a great deal of it; what a queer book it is, and how knowing and deep sometimes amidst what a sea of muddle and platitude I think Goethe must have been asleep when he wrote it: but 'tis a great work somehow. . . .

 . . . A month yesterday we left London, and 3 weeks tomorrow we came here: I have some hopes that we shall be at home again in 3 weeks from today, but don't like to think too much about it; though I catch myself now and then looking at the time-tables and considering which train we shall go to Cologne by: I get out for a walk every morning now, and if the weather looks well stretch my legs a bit, but always take my pocketbook with me and do a little work. . . . I also brought Paris' Death [in *The Earthly Paradise*] to an end roughly; again I'm not very sanguine about the merit of it; but I shall get through the work I set myself to do here in some way, and have a month to turn over the first of the tales before I go to press when I come home . . . I have walked a little through the woods (beech mostly) but they are lonely and dismal except in the brightest weather and so precious full of ants . . . item on wet days the slugs there are bigger and uglier than any I have ever seen 4″ long, most of them a brilliant red-lead colour, but some like bad veal with a shell on their backs; the adders are lively too in this wet warm valley: yesterday morning I heard a rustle in the dry leaves behind me and out crept one as long as my umbrella of a yellowish olive colour and wriggled across the path as though he were expected; I kept feeling the legs of my trousers all the way home after that, and feel a little shy of sitting down on green banks now; however they are always wet. Item I never saw anywhere so many jays all round the edges of the woods they are at it all day long. Magnússons saga [the translation of *The Volsunga Saga*] has turned up and I have begun it; it is rather of the monstrous order but I shall go through with it partly to see what there is good in it partly to fill up the time. . . .

'THE GERMAN LESSON', 1869

[Written by Janey] My finger-tips are sound as you see by this – and fit for much more hard labour – I feel that I have not much else about me that is good for anything, but I have a sort of presentiment (though of course you don't believe in such things) that I may make a rapid turn – and feel myself well all of a sudden – and then I have another presentiment that should this change come – all those I now call my Friends would also change – and would not be able to stand me.

QUEEN GUENEVERE, 1858

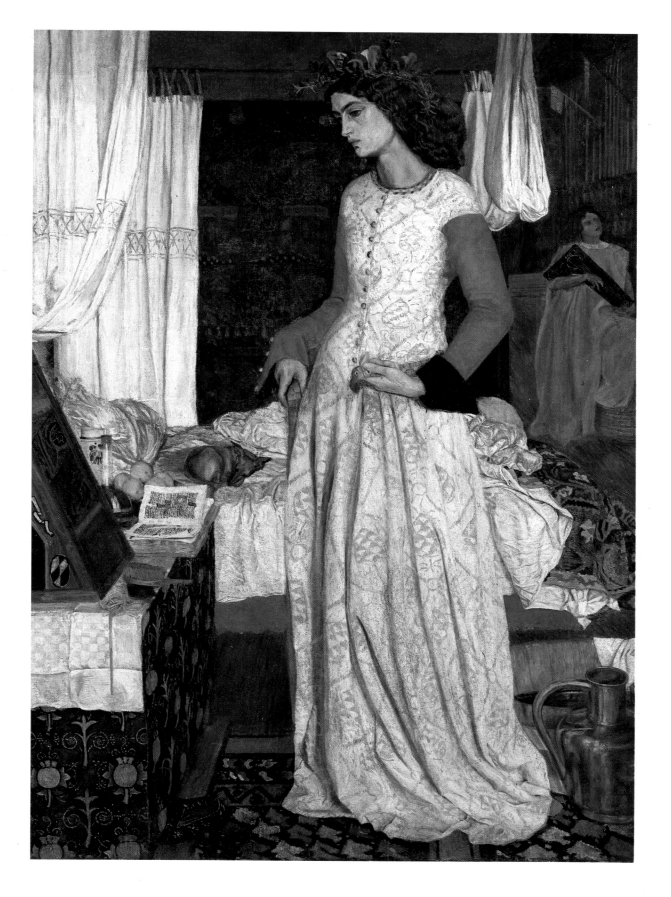

STUDY FOR ISEULT ON THE SHIP, *c.* 1857

CARTOON FOR ARTEMIS, 1861

EMBROIDERED PANELS, 1861

CARTOON FOR ST. PAUL, *c.* 1862

ST. PAUL, 1862

for in him we   live and move and have   our being

STUDY FOR THE VIRGIN OF THE ANNUNCIATION, 1862

THE VIRGIN OF THE ANNUNCIATION, 1862

CARTOON FOR THE ANGEL OF THE ANNUNCIATION, 1862

THE ANGEL OF THE ANNUNCIATION, 1862

CARTOON FOR KING ARTHUR AND SIR LANCELOT, 1862

'IF I CAN' HANGING (DETAIL), *c.* 1857

KING ARTHUR AND SIR LANCELOT

QUEEN GUENEVERE AND ISOUDE LES BLANCHES MAINS

PAINTED PANELS FOR ST. GEORGE'S CABINET, 1862

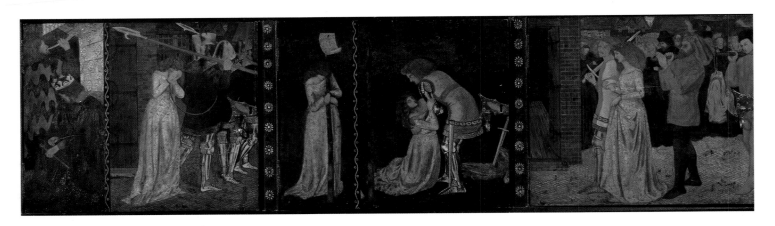

DESIGNS FOR PAINTED PANELS, ST. GEORGE'S CABINET, 1861

DESIGN FOR PAINTED PANELS, ST. GEORGE'S CABINET, 1861

DESIGN FOR TRELLIS WALLPAPER, 1862

TRELLIS WALLPAPER, 1862, IN THE LOBBY, STANDEN

DAISY WALLPAPER, 1862

DAISY HANGING, 1860

CARTOON FOR ARCHANGEL
RAPHAEL, *c.* 1862

ST. MICHAEL, ST. RAPHAEL
AND ST. MICHAEL AND
THE DRAGON, 1862

S·ΩICHAEL·ARCHANGELVS·
+IN MEMORY OF JANE BARBER+

S·RAPHAEL·ARCHANGELVS·
+DECEASED JAN·15 1800: JESU MERCY+

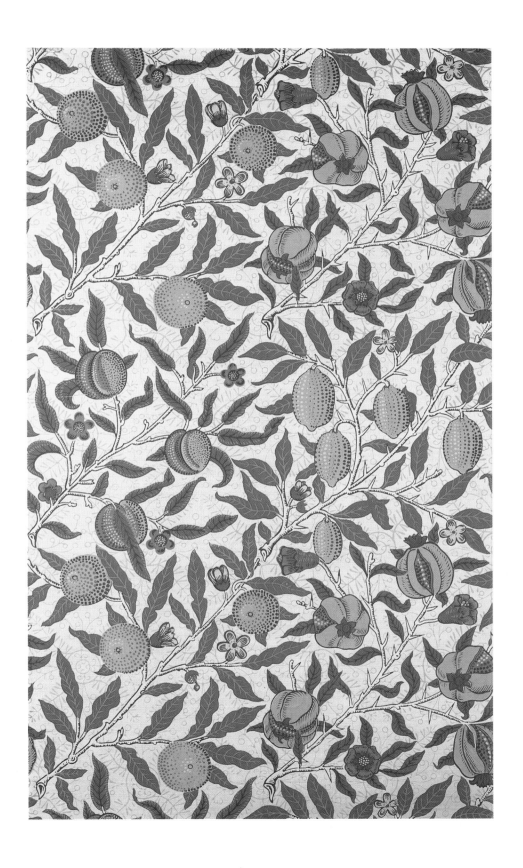

FRUIT (OR POMEGRANATE) WALLPAPER, IN TWO COLOURWAYS, 1864

EAST WINDOW, ALL SAINTS, MIDDLETON CHENEY, NORTHAMPTONSHIRE, 1865

THE ANNUNCIATION, 1865

CARTOON FOR EVE AND THE VIRGIN, *c.* 1865

CARTOON FOR VINE AND GRAPES, 1872—4

NAVE ROOF, JESUS COLLEGE CHAPEL, CAMBRIDGE, *c*. 1866—7

CARTOON FOR ANGEL HOLDING SCROLL, *c.* 1864

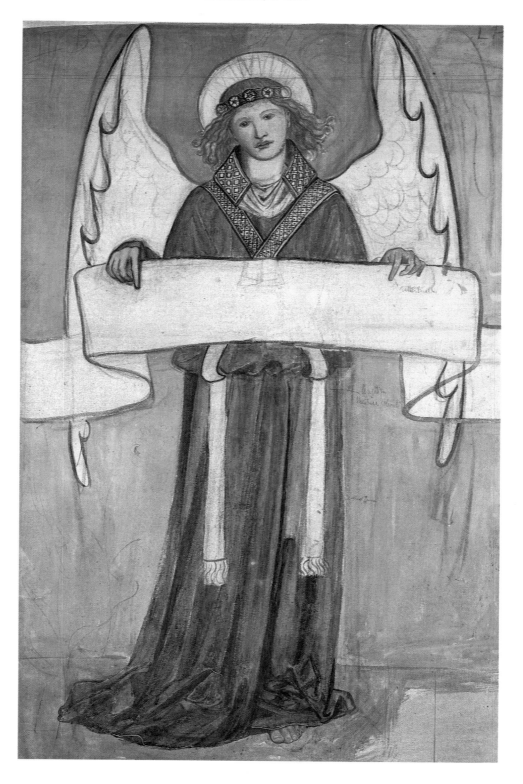

GENERAL VIEW OF QUEENS' COLLEGE HALL, CAMBRIDGE, 1866—7

FIREPLACE TILES, QUEENS' COLLEGE HALL, CAMBRIDGE, 1862−4

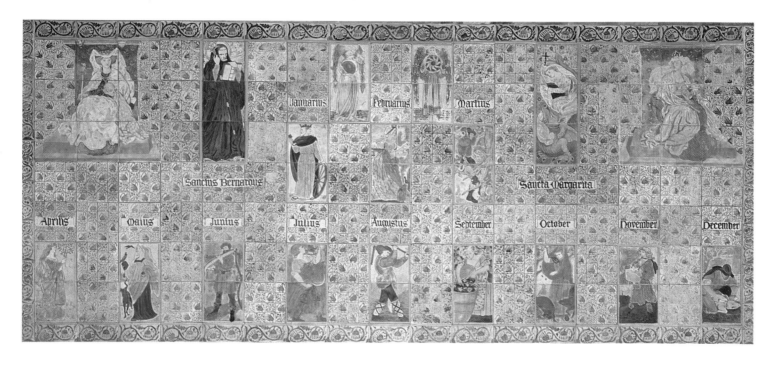

ANGEL WITH VIOLIN, VIRGIN AND CHILD, AND ANGEL
WITH HARP, 1869

ANGEL WITH T-SHAPED DULCIMER, 1869

DETAILS OF ANGELS, 1869

THE THREE MARYS AT THE SEPULCHRE, 1873

EAST WINDOW, ST. MICHAEL, FORDEN, WALES, 1873

THE DWELLERS AT EYR, MANUSCRIPT, c. 1869

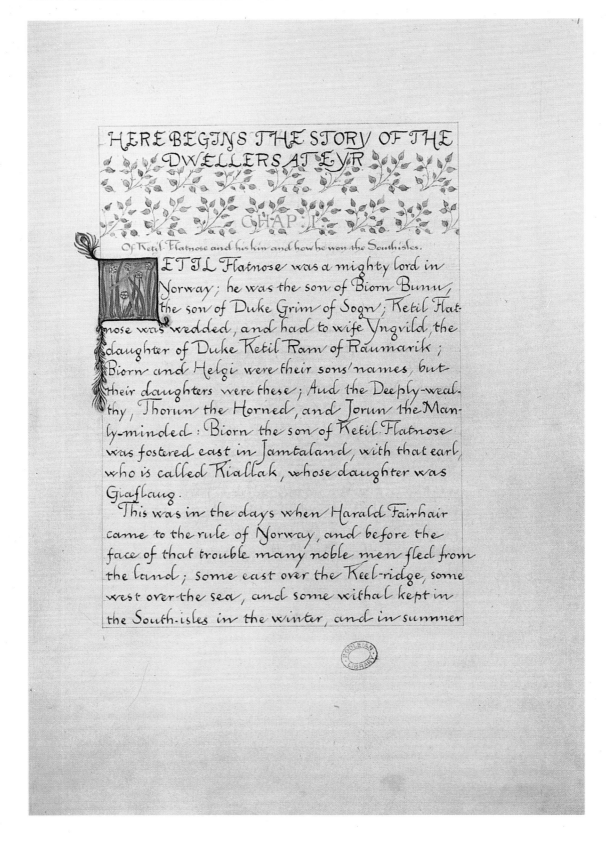

HERE BEGINS THE STORY OF THE DWELLERS AT EYR

CHAP: I.

Of Ketil Flatnose and his kin and how he won the South-isles.

KETIL Flatnose was a mighty lord in Norway; he was the son of Biorn Bunu, the son of Duke Grim of Sogn; Ketil Flatnose was wedded, and had to wife Yngvild, the daughter of Duke Ketil Ram of Raumarik; Biorn and Helgi were their sons' names, but their daughters were these; Aud the Deeply-wealthy, Thorun the Horned, and Jorun the Manly-minded: Biorn the son of Ketil Flatnose was fostered east in Jamtaland, with that earl, who is called Kiallak, whose daughter was Giaflaug.

This was in the days when Harald Fairhair came to the rule of Norway, and before the face of that trouble many noble men fled from the land; some east over the Keel-ridge, some west over the sea, and some withal kept in the South-isles in the winter, and in summer

THE STORY OF THE VOLSUNGS AND THE NIBLUNGS, MANUSCRIPT, c. 1870

ERE BEGINS THE TALE AND TELLS
of a man named Sigi, who was called of
men the son of Odin ; another man withal
is told of, hight Skadi, a great man, and mighty of
his hands, yet was Sigi of more might, and higher
of kin, according to the speech of men of that time.
Now Skadi had a thrall, with whom the story
deals somewhat, Bredi was he hight, and was even
named after that work that he had to do ; in
prowess and might of hand he was equal to men
of more account, yea and better than some thereof.
 Now it is to be told, that on a time Sigi fared to
the hunting of the deer, and the thrall with him;
day-long they hunted till the evening, and when
they gathered their prey together at night-fall, lo
greater and more was that which Bredi had slain,
than was Sigi's prey : which thing misliked him
much, and he said that great wonder it was,
that a very thrall should out-do him in the hunting of deer; so he fell on him, and slew him, and
buried the body of him thereafter in the snow.
Then he went home in the evening, and said
that Bredi had ridden away from him into the
wild-wood : Soon was he out of my sight, says

BROWNING'S *PARACELSUS, c.* 1870

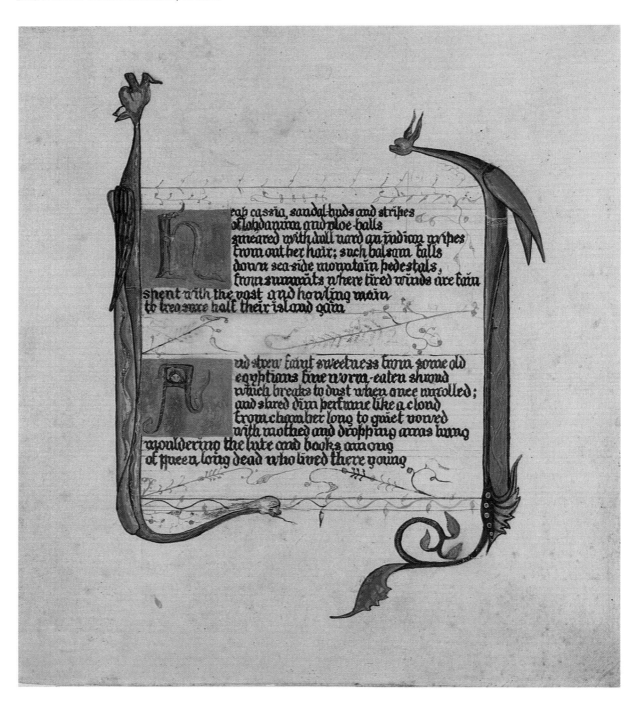

THE EARTHLY PARADISE, c. 1866

The Story of Cupid and Pfyche.

Argument.

Pfyche was a King's daughter, whofe beauty made all people forget Venus, wherefore the Goddefs hated her, and would fain have deftroyed her: neverthelefs fhe became the bride of Love, but her fifters gave her fuch evil counfel that he was wrath with her, and left her: whereon, fhe, having firft revenged herfelf of her fifters, wandered through the world feeking him, and fo doing, fell into the hands of Venus, who tormented her, and fet her fearful tafks to accomplifh; but the Gods and all nature helped her, fo that at laft fhe was reunited to love, forgiven by Venus, and made immortal by the Father of Gods and Men.

Part I.

IN the Greek land of old there was a King [thing,
Happy in battle, rich in every
But chiefly that he had a young daughter [in her,
Who was fo fair all men rejoiced

Pfyche and her beauty.

So fair that ftrangers, landed from the fea,
Beholding her, thought verily that fhe
Was Venus vifible to mortal eyes,
Frefh come from Cyprus for a world's furprife.
She was fo beautiful, that had fhe ftood
On windy Ida by the oaken-wood,
And bared her body to that fhepherd's gaze,
Troy might have ftood till now with happy days,
And thofe three faireft all have gone away
And left her with the apple on that day.

And Pfyche is her name in ftories old
As even by our fathers we were told;
All this faw Venus from her golden throne,
And knew that fhe no longer was alone
For beauty, but, if even for a while

Pfyche hated of Venus.

This damfel matched her God-enticing fmile:
Wherefore fhe wrought in fuch a wife, that fhe,
If honoured as a Goddefs, certainly,

Was dreaded as a Goddefs none the lefs,
And pined away long time in lonelinefs.

Two fifters had fhe, and men called them fair—
But as king's daughters might be anywhere,—
And thefe to lords of great name and eftate
Were wedded, but at home muft Pfyche wait.

Her fifters wedded, but fhe a virgin.

The fons of kings before her filver feet
Still bowed and fighed for her; in mufic fweet
The minftrels to all men ftill fung her praife,
While fhe muft live a virgin all her days.

So to Apollo's temple fent the King
To afk for aid and counfell in this thing,
And therewith fent he goodly gifts of price,
A filken veil wrought with a paradife,

The King fends to the oracle.

Three golden bowls fet round with many a gem,
Three filver cloaks, gold fewn in every hem,
And a fair ivory image of the God
That underfoot a golden ferpent trod:
And when three lords with thefe were gone away
And muft be gone now till the twentieth day,
Ill was the King at eafe, and neither took
Joy in the chafe, nor in the pictured book
The fkilled Athenian limner had juft wrought,
Or in the golden cloths from India brought.
At laft the day came for thofe lords' return,

TWO PAGES FROM *A BOOK OF VERSE,* 1870

LOVE FULFILLED.

HAST thou longed through weary days
For the sight of one loved face,
Hast thou cried aloud for rest,
Mid the pain of sundering hours,
Cried aloud for sleep and death
Since the sweet unhoped for best
Was a shadow and a breath —
O, long now, for no fear lowers
O'er these faint feet-kissing flowers
O, rest now; and yet in sleep
All thy longing shalt thou keep.

Thou shalt rest, and have no fear
Of a dull awaking near,
Of a life for ever blind,
Uncontent and waste and wide.
Thou shalt wake, and think it sweet
That thy love is near and kind
Sweeter still for lips to meet;
Sweetest, that thine heart doth hide
Longing all unsatisfied
With all longing's answering
Howsoever close ye cling

JASMINE TRAIL (OR JASMINE TRELLIS) PRINTED COTTON, 1868–70

KELMSCOTT MANOR

The many-gabled old house

Morris took over the lease of Kelmscott Manor, in the Cotswold village on the Oxfordshire/Gloucestershire borders, in June 1871, at the time he was about to leave on his first trip to Iceland. He originally bought the lease with Rossetti, so that Janey and the girls could spend time there for their health's sake, and (implicit, although never overtly discussed in the correspondence) Rossetti could be with Janey. Rossetti's presence there, needless to say, was irksome to Morris. His letter of 25 November 1872 to Aglaia Coronio is one of the rare available instances when Morris conveys his true feelings about the relationship between Janey and Rossetti, and his personal reliance on friends, especially Georgiana Burne-Jones, to help him through the crisis. Rossetti, however, ended his relationship with Janey in 1874, leaving Morris and his family in possession of the house, which is now tenderly preserved and looked after by the Society of Antiquaries, who furnished it with Morris & Co. designs, and relevant paintings, after his death.

GEORGIANA BURNE-JONES, DATE UNKNOWN

17 MAY 1871

To Charles Faulkner　　　　　　　　　　　　. . . I have been looking about for a house for the wife and kids, and whither do you guess my eye is turned now? Kelmscott, a little village about two miles above Radcott Bridge – a heaven on earth; an old stone Elizabethan house like Water Eaton, and such a garden! close down on the river, a boat house and all things handy. I am going there again on Saturday with Rossetti and my wife: Rossetti because he thinks of sharing it with us if the thing looks likely . . .

AUG.–SEPT. 1871

To unknown recipient　　　　　　　　　　. . . We have taken a little place deep down in the country, where my wife and children are to spend some months every year, as they did this – a beautiful and strangely naïf house, Elizabethan in appearance, though much later in date, as in that out of the way corner people built Gothic till the beginning or middle of the last century. It is on the S.W. extremity of Oxfordshire, within a stone's throw of the baby Thames, in the most beautiful grey little hamlet called Kelmscott.

From News from Nowhere　　　　　　　　. . . The raised way led us into a little field bounded by a backwater of the river on one side; on the right hand we could see a cluster of small houses and barns, new and old, and before us a grey stone barn and a wall partly overgrown with ivy, over which a few grey gables showed. The village road ended in the shadow of the aforesaid backwater. We crossed the road, and again almost against my will my hand raised the latch of a door in the wall, and we stood presently on a stone path which led up to the old house to which fate . . . had so strangely brought me in this new world of men. My companion gave a sigh of pleased surprise and enjoyment; nor did I wonder, for the garden between the wall and the house was redolent of June flowers, and the roses were rolling over one another with that delicious superabundance of small well-tended gardens which at first sight takes away all thought from the beholder save that of beauty. The blackbirds were singing their loudest, the doves were cooing on the roof-ridge, the rooks in the high elm-trees beyond were garrulous among the young leaves, and the swifts wheeled whining about the gables. And the house itself was a fit guardian for all the beauty of this heart of summer.

Once again Ellen echoed my thoughts as she said: 'Yes, friend, this is what I came out for to see; this many-gabled old house built by the simple country-folk of long-past times, regardless of all the turmoil that was going on in cities and courts, is lovely still amidst all the beauty which these latter days have created; and I do not wonder at our friends tending it carefully and making much of it. It seems to me as if it had waited for these happy days, and held in it the gathered crumbs of happiness of the confused and turbulent past.' . . .

We went in, and . . . wandered from room to room . . . to the strange and quaint garrets amongst the great timbers of the roof, where of old time the tillers and herdsmen of the manor slept, but which a-nights seemed now, by the small size of the beds, and the litter of useless and disregarded matters – bunches of dying flowers, feathers of birds, shells of starlings' eggs, caddis worms in mugs and the like – seemed to be inhabited for the time by children.

Everywhere there was but little furniture, and that only the most necessary, and of the

KELMSCOTT MANOR

KELMSCOTT MANOR, OXFORDSHIRE

DRAWING ROOM

THE ATTIC ROOM

BEDROOM

WATERCOLOUR OF KELMSCOTT MANOR

simplest forms. The extravagant love of ornament which I had noted in this people elsewhere seemed here to have given place to the feeling that the house itself and its associations was the ornament of the country life amidst which it had been left stranded from old times, and that to re-ornament it would but take away its use as a piece of natural beauty.

We sat down at last in a room . . . which was still hung with old tapestry, originally of no artistic value, but now faded into pleasant grey tones which harmonized thoroughly well with the quiet of the place, and which would have been ill supplanted by brighter and more striking decoration.

8 OCT. 1872

To Aglaia Coronio . . . I have been backwards and forwards to Kelmscott a great deal this summer and autumn; but should not go there so often now as Gabriel is come there, and talks of staying there permanently – of course he won't do that, but I suppose he will stay some time – he is quite well and seems very happy . . .

QUEEN SQUARE, 25 NOV. 1872

. . . One thing wanting ought not to go for so much – nor indeed does it spoil my enjoyment of life always, as I have often told you: to have real friends and some sort of aim in life is so much, that I ought still to think myself lucky – and often in my better moods I wonder what it is in me that throws me into such rage and despair at other times; I suspect, do you know, that some such moods would have come upon me at times even without this failure of mine. However that may be though I must confess that this autumn has been a specially dismal time with me – I have been a good deal in the house here – not alone, that would have been pretty well, – but alone with poor Bessy [Janey's sister]: I must say it is a shame, she is quite harmless and even good, and one ought not to be irritated with her – but O my God what I have suffered from finding [her] always there at meals and the like! poor soul 'tis only because she is an accidental person with whom I have nothing whatever to do: I am so glad to have Janey back again – her company is always pleasant and she is very kind and good to me – furthermore my intercourse with G. [Georgiana] has been a good deal interrupted not from any coldness of hers or violence of mine; but from so many untoward nothings: then you have been away so that I have had nobody to talk to about things that bothered me – which I repeat I have felt more than I, in my ingratitude, expected to. Another quite selfish business is that Rossetti has set himself down at Kelmscott as if he never meant to go away; and not only does that keep me away from the harbour of refuge (because it really is a farce our meeting when we can help it) but also he has all sorts of ways so unsympathetic with the sweet simple old place, that I feel his presence there is a kind of slur on it – this is very unreasonable though when one thinks why one took the place, and how this year it has really answered that purpose: nor do I think that I would feel this way about it if he had not been so unromantically discontented with it & the whole thing which made me very angry and dissappointed – There, dear Aglaia see how I am showing my pettinesses! *please* don't encourage me in them; but you have always been so kind to me that they will come out. O how I long to keep the world from narrowing in on me, and to look at things bigly and kindly!

I am going to try to get to Iceland next year, hard as it will be to drag myself away from two or three people in England; but I know there will be a kind of rest in it, let alone the help it will bring me from physical reasons; I know clearer now perhaps than then what a blessing & help last year's journey was to me; or what horrors it saved me from. But if I can't go, I shall have a fortnight or so on the river as a pis aller . . .

Forgive my rambling and most egotistical letter.

16 APRIL 1874

To Dante Gabriel Rossetti   I send herewith the £17 10 [the rent] to you, not knowing where else to send it since Kinch [probably the managing agent] is dead. As to the future though I will ask you to look upon me as off my share, & not to look upon me as shabby for that, since you have taken to fairly living at Kelmscott, which I suppose neither of us thought the other would do when we first began the possession of the house; for the rest I am both too poor &, by compulsion of poverty, too busy to be able to use it much in any case, and am very glad you will find it useful and pleasant to you.

KELMSCOTT MANOR, 9 JULY 1876

To Janey   Here I am then all safe: I have passed the morning on the river – the fishing is bad; water low and bright – but I am not absolutely fishless, even as you foretold: for I am to dine off fish today, and am sousing (or Mrs. Comely [housekeeper] is) two small jack for tomorrow or Sunday. The morning was not unpleasant, but this afternoon has turned out diabolically so – a strong East wind & a yellow blight are depressing even at Kelmscott – Ah, it is raining fast now, which I am glad of, as we may have a change tomorrow. The garden has suffered here much from the cold & wet, I mean to say as to vegetable, for it looks beautiful – the strawberry bed is a mass of blossoms; there [are] no roses out except the yellow ones on the gable wall of the barn; but a fortnight hence

'ENTER MORRIS, MOORED IN A PUNT,
AND JACKS & TENCHES EXEUNT', 1871

it will be a wonder for the roses; I must try to get down even for a day at that time . . .

I shall not come back till Wednesday if all bowls row aright – I enjoyed my morning on the river very much, though I lost the only good perch I hooked, by my own stupidity, also by the same course of action a big chub.

To Georgiana [*Burne-Jones*]   Somehow I feel as if there must soon be an end to me of playing at living in the country: a town-bird I am, a master artisan, if I might claim that latter dignity.

. . . I am sitting now, 10 p.m., in the tapestry room, the moon rising red through the east-wind haze out of the river, and a cow lowing over the fields. I have been feeling chastened by many thoughts, and the beauty and quietness of the surroundings, which latter, as I hinted, I am, as it were, beginning to take leave of. That leave-taking will, I confess, though you may think it fantastic, seem a long step towards saying good night to the world.

Most strange and awful the country

Morris first went to Iceland in 1871 with Eiríkr Magnússon, who had taught him Icelandic, and collaborated with his translations of the Sagas. His old friend Charlie Faulkner also went with him (according to May Morris, Faulkner was far from well at the time, and suffered terribly from sea-sickness, and the rigours of the journey). The fourth member of the party was W.H. Evans, an ex-army officer who contacted Morris when he heard about the voyage, and who went along for the shooting and the fishing. The expedition lasted two months; most of the journey was done on horseback, and Morris acted as cook. He recorded events and his impressions in a journal, which was probably written for Georgiana Burne-Jones. He returned to Iceland in 1873 (when Rossetti was again at Kelmscott); his records of this second journey are far less copious, however, and they have not been included in this selection.

From Poems by the Way

'Iceland First Seen'

Ah! What came we forth for to see
that our hearts are so hot with desire?
Is it enough for our rest,
the sight of this desolate strand,
And the mountain waste voiceless as death
but for winds that sleep not nor tire?
Why do we long to wend forth

Through the length and breadth of a land,
Dreadful with grinding of ice,
and record of scarce hidden fire,
But that there 'mid the grey grassy dales
sore scarred by the ruining streams
Lives the tale of the Northland of old
and the undying glory of dreams?

To Edith Mary Story   . . . I am going [on] what to me is a long journey this year; you in the middle of all your works of art and the luxury of a beautiful climate will shudder at my choice I fancy: still one will always be ready to go to Italy while the possibility of driving oneself to *Iceland* may fail one: for I am really going there this summer: there is no art there at all, and there is nothing to interest most people there but its strangeness and wildness; yet I have felt for long that I must go there and see the background of the stories for wh: I have so much sympathy and which must have had something to do with producing and fostering their strange imagination: also to such a cockney stay at home as I am there is a certain amount of adventure about the journey which pleases me . . .

'WILLIAM MORRIS ON HORSEBACK IN ICELAND', 1870

MAY 1871

To Charles Faulkner   Don't forget to practice riding. I began this morning. By Gum the great we shall have plenty of it there according to our programme.

From Morris's journal   [Sunday 9 July, on board *Diana* somewhere in the Pentland Firth] . . . nine o'clock was breakfast proper, by which time we were getting off the firth and she was beginning to roll, for which she had a great talent; nevertheless I sat down to breakfast with a huge appetite . . . breakfast was beefsteak and onions, smoked salmon, Norway anchovies, hard-boiled eggs, cold meat, cheese and radishes and butter, all very plenteous: this was the regular breakfast, only varied by bacon and eggs instead of beef. Faulkner looked serious as he sat down and presently disappeared; I think the first man on board . . .

[Tuesday 11 July, landing on the Faroe Islands, 200 miles north-west of the Shetlands] . . . we turned a corner of the stony stepped grey hills, and below us lay a deep, calm sound, say two miles broad, a hog-backed steep mountain island forming the other side of it, next to which lay a steeper islet, a mere rock; and then the other islands, the end of which we could not see, entangled the sound; I was most deeply impressed with it all, yet can scarcely tell you why; it was like nothing I had ever seen, but strangely like my old imaginations of places for sea-wanderers to come to.

[Thursday 13 July, on board *Diana* off the coast of Rangarvalla-sysla, Iceland] . . . and on our left was a dark brown ragged rocky island, Pápey, and many small skerries about, and beyond that we saw the mainland, a terrible shore indeed! a great mass of dark grey mountains worked into pyramids and shelves, looking as if they had been built half-ruined; they were striped with snow high up and wreaths of cloud dragged across them here and there, and above them were two peaks and a jagged ridge of pure white snow.

[Saturday 15 July, at Reykjavik] Evans and I bought some stores at the Cooperative in the Haymarket . . . a parcel not ours came in the cases, instead of some bologna sausage we had ordered . . . I suggested (as the wildest possible idea) fragrant Floriline [a scented mouthwash] and hair brushes – in went the chisel, and off came the lid: there was the side of bacon; there were the tins of preserved meat; there was the Liebig, the soup-squares, the cocoa, the preserved carrots and the peas and sage and onions & here IT is – four boxes of fragrant Floriline . . .

We looked at each other to see if we were drunk or dreaming, and then – to say we laughed – how does that describe the row we made; we were on the edge of the hayfield at the back of the house; the haymakers ran up and leaned on their rakes & looked at us amazed and half-frightened; man, woman and child ran from their houses, to see what was toward; but all shame and care had left us and there we rolled about and roared until nature refused to help us any longer!

To Janey

Well, my dear, here I am safe & quite well . . . all goes well and we start up country tomorrow with 20 horses, such jolly little fellows the poneys are; they almost look as if they would talk . . . on Tuesday morning about seven we reached Thorshaven [Thörshavn] in the Faroes, and went ashore for 12 hours: we went a long walk over the hills on the most beautiful of days and it was so calm that evening that the captain was able to thread the labyrinth of the islands, and a most wonderful sight it was: I have seen nothing out of a dream so strange as our coming out of the last narrow sound into the Atlantic, and leaving the huge wall of rocks astern in the shadowless midnight twilight; nothing I have ever seen has impressed me so much . . . on Thursday morning about 3 Mag.[nússon] called me up to see Iceland . . . it is no use trying to describe it, but it was quite up to my expectations as to strangeness: it is just like nothing else in the world . . .

. . . We got to Reykjavik about 3 in the afternoon this day (Friday) and went ashore soon, and were taken by Mag. to the house of one of his kinsfolk and are quite comfortable a-night on the floor a very small clean room, and are abundantly fed: the town itself might be in Canada and is quite commonplace, but all the houses are quite clean – inside . . .

'MORRIS HAS COME BACK FROM ICELAND MORE ENSLAVED WITH A PASSION FOR ICE AND SNOW AND RAW FISH THAN EVER', 1870

REYKJAVIK, 16 JULY 1871

To Jenny and May [*daughters*] Isn't it funny that I am writing to you from Iceland . . . we had a good voyage, and I was not very sick: one day we saw porpoises a long way off and when they saw the ship they swam after it as fast as they could, jumping out of the water so that you could see them all: they soon came up with the ship and played about her – it made one laugh so, because they looked like oiled pigs . . .

I hope you are very good and kind to Mama and that you are happy at Kelmscott: it is not much like Iceland I can tell you. I send you some wild thyme I plucked this morning in the fields close by here: there are many pretty flowers about, but no trees at all; not even a bush about here, but the mountains are very beautiful.

From Morris's journal [Monday 17 July, from Reykjavik to Bergthorsknoll and Lithend] Most strange and awful the country looked to me as we passed through, in spite of all my anticipations: a doleful land at first, with its great rubbish heaps of sand, striped scantily with grass sometimes; varied though by a band of sweet grass here & there full of flowers, and little willowy grey leaved plants that I can't name: till at last we came to our first river that runs through a soft grassy plain into a bright bight of the firth; it is wonderfully clear – its flowery green lips seemed quite beautiful to me in the sunny evening, though I think that at any time I should have liked the place, with the grass and the sea and the river all meeting, and the great black mountain (Esja) on the other side of the firth.

'WILLIAM MORRIS CLIMBING A MOUNTAIN IN ICELAND', 1870

[Tuesday 25 July, in camp at Geysir]...We can see the low crater of the big Geysir now quite clearly...and presently...came right on the beastly place...and rode off the turf onto the sulphurous accretions formed by the overflow, which is even now trickling over it, warm enough to make our horses snort and plunge with terror; so on to a piece of turf about twenty yards from the tip of the crater...the turf is the only nasty piece of camping ground we have had yet, all bestrewn with feathers and wings of birds, polished mutton bones, and above all pieces of paper ...

[Tuesday 1 Aug., in the bonder's house at Grímstunga] I did fairly go to sleep on the road, and fell to dreams of people at home...I was woke up by a halt, and Magnússon coming to tell me that my little haversack was missing: now in that said haversack I had the notes of this present journal; pipe, spare spectacles, drawing materials, and other things I didn't want to lose, so I hope to be forgiven if I confess I lost my temper, and therefore threatened to kill Eyvindr, to whom I had given it...he, poor fellow, answered not, but caught an empty horse and set off through the storm.

[Sunday 6 Aug., in camp in the home-mead of Herdholt]...Yet it is an awful place: set aside the hope that the unseen sea gives you here, and the strange threatening change of the blue spiky mountains beyond the firth, and the rest seems emptiness and nothing else: a piece of turf under your feet, and the sky overhead, that's all;

whatever solace your life is to have here must come out of yourself or these old stories, not over hopeful in themselves.

[Thursday 10 Aug., at Mr Thorlacius's house at Stykkishólm] . . . As we rode along the winding path we saw a strange sight: a huge eagle quite within gunshot of us, and not caring at all for that, flew across and across our path, always followed by a raven that seemed to be teazing and buffetting him: this was the first eagle that I had ever seen free and on the wing, and it was a glorious sight, no less; the curves of his flight, as he swept close by us, with every pen of his wings clear against the sky was a sight never to be forgotten . . .

[Wednesday 16 Aug., in camp in the home-stead of Staðastaör] I dreamed very distinctly this morning that I had come home again, and that Webb was asking me what sort of climate we had in Iceland; I cried out 'atrocious' and waking therewith heard the rain pattering on the tent . . . I lay for some time puzzled to think where I was, and with an unhappy feeling of being a long way from where I wanted to be, and there and then began an access of home-sickness for me. . . .

[Monday 21 Aug., in camp in the home-mead at Stafholt] . . . So to bed in our tent, where in the dead of night C.F.J. and I quarrelled in this wise; I who upon my honour was lying awake, heard him snoring violently, but bore it well for a time, till it rose to a roaring, snuffling climax, and I thought I should go mad, and shouted out 'damn!'. This woke C.F.J., who said, as if he had never been asleep in his life, and in a disagreeable tone of voice just as if he were seeking out a quarrel,

'What's the matter now?'

Justly indignant at this speech & the tone of it, I said rather hotly 'You were snoring like the devil'.

He said in almost unpleasant tone, as if I *must* always be in the wrong, 'I have been awake for half an hour.'

I (still indignant, but willing in my good nature to give him a loop-hole for escape), 'You must have been snoring awake then, and I wish the devil you wouldn't'.

He (sourly and obstinately), 'It so happens that I particularly noticed that I was awake, for I was thinking that the wind was getting up & that it might rain in the night, and that I had better move the things from the tent walls.'

I (rather hotly for I was getting roused), 'Why did you snore then?'

He, 'I didn't.'

I, 'You did.'

He 'it was you who were snoring and dreamed it was I.'

Indignation should have kept me silent after this, but I thought it disrespectful not to answer an old friend, so I exerted myself to say: 'It so happens that I particularly noticed that I was awake, for I was just thinking of getting up to move the gun-case away from the tent walls.'

He (most disagreeably) 'Rubbish'.

Speechless indignation now indeed: and so to sleep.

[Tuesday 22 Aug., in the priest's house at Gilsbank] But waking this morning it occurred to me that something amusing had happened, without remembering what it was at first, till at last it smote upon me & I fell a roaring with laughter, as did C.F.J. no less and no later; so small a joke moving our little minds in those waste places — owing to the fresh air?

[Friday 25 Aug., in camp in the home-mead of Thingvellir] . . . My heart beats, so please you, as we near the brow of the pass, and all the infinite wonder, which came upon me when I came up on the deck of the 'Diana' to see Iceland for the first time, comes upon me again now, for this is the heart of Iceland that we are going to see: nor was the reality of the sight unworthy; the pass showed long and winding from the brow, with jagged dark hills showing over the nearer banks of it as you went on, and betwixt them was an open space with a great unseen but imagined plain between you and the great lake that you saw far away under huge peaked hills of bright blue with grey-green sky above them, Hengill the highest of them, from the hot spring on whose flank rose into the air a wavering column of snow white steam . . .

[Thursday 7 Sept., in England again] . . . So there I was in London at last, well washed, and finding nobody I cared for dead: a piece of luck that does not always happen to people when they are fools enough to go away beyond call for more than two months . . .

KELMSCOTT, 18 SEPT. 1871

To his mother
I am back here safe and sound . . . we had a very successful trip, all things considered, and I am as well as a man can be: all is well here & the place looking beautiful . . . I won't say any more about my tour till I see you, except that it has done me a world of good both mind and body . . .

QUEEN SQUARE, 19 OCT. 1871

To Charles Eliot Norton
. . . Am I to defend myself for going to Iceland instead of Italy? I can only say in these matters one must follow ones instinct & mine drove me there: you see the change of life was complete: we were 6 weeks in the saddle: on 24 nights I slept in a tent: I got quite knowing about horses: I acquired a competent knowledge of that useful art of *cookery* — under difficulties too, I can tell you — for I was master cook to the company. — don't you remember our argument about servants, at the Grange one night, & how I thought them immoral (the use of them I mean) — well here we were without them: for though our guides Gisti and Eyrvidr were engaged to serve us by day yet they worked no harder than we, except where their knowledge was special, and they paid us no sort of defference except that of good-fellowship . . . Then the people: lazy, dreamy, without enterprise or hope: awfully poor, and used to all kinds of privations — and with all that, gentle, kind, intensely curious, full of their old lore, living in their stirring past . . . Truly it would have been all nothing but for the memory of the old story tellers; nay I think without them the people would have long ago sunk into stolidity and brutality — yet it was all enjoyment . . .

COMMITMENT

The Eastern Question

William Morris showed no overt interest in politics until the autumn of 1876, when he threw himself into the furore that was precipitated by Disraeli's support for the Turks in their conflict with Bulgarian nationalists. In June 1876 Turkish mercenaries had savagely attacked and suppressed the Christian population in Bulgaria who were protesting against Turkish rule. Disraeli, then prime minister and leader of the Tory party, supported the Turks in the interest of both trade and the balance of power . . . he needed a strong and friendly Turkey to protect the newly opened Suez Canal, and to counter the threat of Russian expansion in the Balkans. The Russians, according to the Tory party, were waiting in the wings, and their threats to oust the Turks from Bulgaria were strategic rather than humanitarian. Gladstone, leader of the Liberals, who had retired from politics following his defeat in the General Election of 1874, took this as an opportunity to return to the fray, claiming that decency and humanity should take precedence over expediency.

Morris's politics, prior to this, had been vaguely Liberal. It is interesting to note, however, that in his letter to Andreas Scheu of September 1883 (see pages 15–17) he dates his awareness of the class struggle to the first visit to Iceland: 'In 1871 I went to Iceland with Mr Magnússon, and apart from my pleasure in seeing that romantic desert, I learned one lesson there, thoroughly I hope, that the most grinding poverty is a trifling evil compared with the inequality of the classes.'

QUEEN SQUARE, 24 OCT. 1876

To the Editor, The Daily News   'England and the Turks'

I cannot help noting that a rumour is about in the air that England is going to war; and from the depths of my astonishment I ask, On behalf of whom? Against whom? And for what end? Some three weeks ago, if such a rumour had arisen, my questions would, I imagine, have been answered in this way:– 'The English nation has been roused to a sense of justice (for at heart they are a generous people) by a story of horrors that no man has been able to gainsay; so they are going to war against the Turkish government on behalf of certain subject peoples, whom the Turks conquered long ago but have never assimilated, and whom now, in their decrepitude, insolvency, and terror, they have been torturing and oppressing in the vilest manner, while they claim to be considered and treated as a civilized Government and a part of the comity of Europe. The end and aim of the war is to force the Turkish government (who, to speak the downright truth, are a gang of thieves and murderers) to give these subject peoples, who are quite orderly and industrious, some chance for existence . . . and we and all Europe think that it is a just and honourable aim, and that we are the right people to see it carried through; for we, a peaceful people, not liars (except in trade), we have nothing to gain by helping these luckless folk to live . . .'

 . . . And now, not even the wretched packed Parliament we have is sitting. The cry for

'THE BURNING AND SACK OF BATAK', 1876

that was not believed; the members are too busy shooting in the country, and the nation is dumb, if it were not for the 2,000 working men who met last Sunday at Clerkenwell, and who took it for granted, as everybody else I come across does, that the crossing of the Turkish boundaries by Russian troops would be followed at greater or less time by England's declaration of war against Russia. And do you not suppose that the Turks do not take the same thing for granted?

I appeal to the Liberal Party, and ask if it is not worth while their making some effort to avoid this shame. I appeal to the working men, and pray them to look to it that if this shame falls upon them they will certainly remember it and be burdened by it when their day clears for them, and they attain all, and more than all, they now are striving for; to the organizers of both these bodies I specially appeal . . . no war on behalf of Turkey: no war on behalf of the thieves and murderers! I appeal to all men of sense and feeling of all parties, and bid them think what war means, and to think that if only perhaps this were an unjust war! What, then, would come of it but shame in defeat and shame in victory, and in the end ignominious undoing of all that the war should seem to do. I who am writing this am one of a large class of men – quiet men, who usually go about their own business, heeding public matters less than they ought, and afraid to speak in such a huge concourse as the English nation, however much they may feel, but who are now stung into bitterness by thinking how helpless they are in a public matter that touches them so closely. To these also I appeal to break silence at last . . .

I beg with humility to be allowed to inscribe myself, in the company of Mr Gladstone, and Mr Freeman and all men that I esteem, as an hysterical sentimentalist; and am, Sir, your obedient servant. . . .

4 MAY 1877

To Georgiana   I was at the working-men's meeting at the Cannon Street Hotel on Wednesday, it was quite a success; they seem to have advanced since last autumn. Some of them spoke very well . . . Burt (M.P. for Morpeth, who is, or was, a working man) was chairman, and spoke excellently though shortly, with a strong Northumberland tongue; he seemed a capital fellow. Meantime the Liberal party is blown to pieces, and everything is in confusion.

From Unjust War   To the Working-men of England

Friends and fellow-citizens,

There is danger of war; bestir yourselves to face that danger: if you go to sleep, saying we do not understand it, and the danger is far off, you may wake and find the evil fallen upon you, for even now it is at the door. . . . We shall pay heavily, and you, friends of the working-classes, will pay the heaviest.

And what shall we buy at this heavy price? Will it be glory, and wealth and peace for those that come after us? Alas! no; for these are the gains of a *just* war; but if we wage the *unjust* war that fools and cowards are bidding us wage to-day, our loss of wealth will buy us fresh losses of wealth, our loss of work will buy us loss of hope, our loss of friends and kindred will buy us enemies from father to son.

An unjust war, I say: for do not be deceived! if we go to war with Russia now, it will not be to punish her for evil deeds done, or to hinder her from evil deeds hereafter, but to put down just insurrection against the thieves and murderers of Turkey; to stir up a faint pleasure in the hearts of the do-nothing fools that cry out without meaning for a 'spirited foreign policy'; to guard our well-beloved rule in India from the coward fear of an invasion that may happen a hundred years hence – or never; to exhibit our army and navy once more before the wondering eyes of Europe; to give a little hope to our holders of Turkish bonds: – Working-men of England, which of these things do you think worth starving for, worth dying for? Do all of them rolled into one make that body of *English Interests* we have heard of lately?

And who are they who flaunt in our faces the banner inscribed on one side *English Interests*, and on the other *Russian Misdeeds*? Who are they that are leading us into war? Let us look at these saviours of England's honour, these champions of Poland, these scourges of Russia's iniquities! Do you know them? – Greedy gamblers on the Stock Exchange, idle officers of the army and navy (poor fellows!) worn-out mockers of the Clubs, desperate purveyors of exciting war-news for the comfortable breakfast tables of those who have nothing to lose by war, and lastly, in the place of honour, the Tory Rump, that we fools, weary of peace, reason and justice, chose at the last election to 'represent' us. . . .

19 JAN. 1878

To Janey   . . . As to the agitation: I must confess I have been agitated as well as agitating: . . . the little meeting was noisy, but I call it a success considering the slight care with which it was got up: at least it quite refused to cheer the Empress Brown [Queen Victoria]: you see I had to speak at the end, by which time the peace-party desired to fight for peace, and the war-party was blue with rage. The evening meeting was magnificent – orderly and enthusiastic, though mind you, it took some very heavy work to keep the enemies roughs out: and the noise of them outside was like the sea roaring against a lighthouse . . . you will have seen about our music – wasn't it a good idea? ['Wake London Lads'] . . . they set me to write the song, which I did on Monday night. It went down very well, & they sang it well together: they struck up when we were just ready to come on to the platform & you may imagine I felt rather excited when I heard them begin to tune up – they stopped at the end of each verse and cheered lustily . . .

. . . I am very tired with it and shall enjoy a week of dyeing and designing next week if Dizzy [Disraeli] will let me have it . . .

from 'Wake London Lads' (to be sung to the tune of 'The Hardy Norseman's Home of Yore').

'UNJUST WAR' LETTER, WILLIAM MORRIS, 1876

1. Wake, London Lads, wake, bold and free!
     Arise, and fall to work,
   Lest England's glory come to be
     Bond-servant to the Turk!
   Think of your Sires! how oft and oft
     On freedom's field they bled,
   When Cromwell's hand was raised aloft,
     And Kings and scoundrels fled.

2. From out the dusk, from out the dark,
     Of old our fathers came,
   Till lovely freedom's glimmering spark
     Broke forth a glorious flame:
   And shall we now praise freedom's dearth
     And rob the years to come,
   And quench upon a brother's hearth
     The fires we lit at home? . . .

5. What! shall we crouch beneath the load,
     And call the labour sweet,
   And, dumb and blind, go down the road
     Where shame abides our feet?
   Wake, London Lads! the hour draws nigh,
     The bright sun brings the day;
   Cast off the shame, cast off the lie,
     And cast the Turk away!

1 FEB. 1878

To Janey

. . . our people are much dispirited with the defeat at Sheffield, and the row yesterday in the city [anti-war meetings disrupted by 'war-party rough-necks'], at which latter place there were some 7000 people – they behaved disgracefully, as you will see in the newspapers: they had 400 roughs down in waggons from Woolich Dockyard, & generally played the gooseberry: people on our side had to hide away in cellars and places & get out anyhow: all of this is very enraging, & I am beginning to say, well if they will have war let them fill their bellies with it then! . . . I feel very low and muddled about it all . . .

To Jenny

11 FEB. 1878

. . . the worst part of it all is that the war fever is raging in England, & the people go about in a Rule Britannia style that turns one's stomach . . .

To Janey

20 FEB. 1878

. . . As to my political career, I think that it is at an end for the present; & has ended sufficiently disgustingly, after beating about the bush & trying to organize some rags of resistance to the war-party for a fortnight, after spending all ones time in Committees and the like; I went to Gladstone . . . to talk about getting him to a meeting at the Agricultural Hall: he agreed and was quite hot about it, and as brisk as a bee: I went off strait to the Hall, and took it for tomorrow . . . but – on Monday, our parliamentaries began to quake, and tease Gladstone, and they have quaked the meeting out now – the EQA was foremost in the flight, & really I must needs say they have behaved ill in the matter: Gladstone was quite ready to come up to the scratch & has behaved well throughout – but I am that ashamed that I can scarcely look people in the face though I did my best to keep the thing up: the working men are in a great rage about it, as well they may be . . . there was a stormy meeting of the EQA yesterday, full of wretched little personalities, but I held my tongue – I am out of it now: I mean as to bothering my head about it: I shall give up reading the Papers, and shall stick to my work . . .

To A.J. Mundella

21 MAY 1880

. . . I wonder sometimes as I walk through the streets and look at the people if they are the same flesh & blood as made things so pleasant for us in the spring of '78; and I feel inclined to say, what the deuce then *was* it all about? . . .

Anti-Scrape

At the same time that Morris became involved with politics and the Eastern Association, he launched his attack on current practices of 'restoring' cathedrals and churches, as well as other ancient buildings. His first broadside, a letter to The Athenaeum, *led to the formation of the Society for the Protection of Ancient Buildings – or 'Anti-Scrape', as Morris called it, with Morris as secretary.*

This campaign was not confined to the British Isles. In the autumn of 1879 Morris learned of proposals for a large-scale reconstruction of St Mark's in Venice. Morris, through the SPAB, initiated the protests in England, and he wrote a series of letters about it, to Ruskin, Robert Browning

'THE MORRIS DANCE ROUND ST. MARK'S,' 1880

and Gladstone, as well as to various English and Italian newspapers. A year later, in 1880, the SPAB took up the cause of the Baptistery in Ravenna, which was subsiding.

The Society is still active in Britain today, and Morris's manifesto is still used.

QUEEN SQUARE, 5 MAR. 1877

To the Editor, The Athenaeum   My eye just now caught the word 'restoration' in the morning paper, and, on looking closer, I saw that this time it is nothing less than the Minster of Tewkesbury that is to be destroyed by Sir Gilbert Scott [architect]. Is it altogether too late to do something to save it – it and whatever else of beautiful or historical is still left us on the sites of the ancient buildings we were once so famous for? Would it not be of some use once for all, and with the least delay possible, to set on foot an association for the purpose of watching over and protecting these relics, which, scanty as they are now become, are still wonderful treasures, all the more priceless in this age of the world, when the newly-invented study of living history is the chief joy of so many of our lives?

. . . there are many thoughtful people who would be glad to sacrifice time, money, and comfort in defence of those ancient monuments: besides, though I admit that the architects are, with very few exceptions, hopeless, because interest, habit, and ignorance bind them, and that the clergy are hopeless, because their order, habit, and an ignorance yet grosser, bind them; still there must be many people whose ignorance is accidental rather than inveterate, whose good sense could surely be touched if it were clearly put to them that they were destroying what they, or, more surely still, their sons and sons' sons, would one day fervently long for, and which no wealth or energy could ever buy again for them. . . .

25 MAR. 1877

To Thomas Wardle   We held the first meeting of the Society for the Protection of Ancient Buildings at Queen Sq. on Thursday last, at which I was appointed Honorary Secretary; and I with Webb and George [Wardle] are to draw up a programme setting forth our views and aims, to submit to a meeting on Thursday next; the said programme having been agreed upon we shall ask the world in general to join. I think we shall make the programme explicit enough to keep out pretenders . . . I really do hope we may do something, if only to make the architects a little more careful: my word, but they will be in a rage, if I have my way about the programme!

From 'The Manifesto of

The Society for the Protection of Ancient Buildings'   . . . No doubt within the last fifty years a new interest, almost like another sense, has arisen in these ancient monuments of art; and they have become the subject of one of the most interesting of studies, and of an enthusiasm, religious, historical, artistic, which is one of the undoubted gains of our time; yet we think that if the present treatment of them be continued, our descendants will find them useless for study and chilling to enthusiasm. We think that those last fifty years of knowledge and attention have done more for their destruction than all the foregoing centuries of revolution, violence, and contempt.

For Architecture, long decaying, died out, as a popular art at least, just as the knowledge of mediaeval art was born. So that the civilized world of the nineteenth century has no style of its own amidst its wide knowledge of the styles of other centuries. From this lack and this gain arose in men's minds the strange idea of the Restoration of ancient buildings; and a strange and most fatal idea, which by its very name implies that it is possible to strip from a building this, that, and the other part of its history – of its life that is – and then to stay the hand at some arbitrary point, and leave it still historical, living, and even as it once was.

In early times this kind of forgery was impossible, because knowledge failed the builders, or perhaps because instinct held them back. If repairs were needed, if ambition or piety pricked on to change, that change was of necessity wrought in the unmistakable fashion of the time; a church of the eleventh century might be added to or altered in the twelfth, thirteenth, fourteenth, fifteenth, sixteenth, or even the seventeenth or eighteenth centuries; but every change, whatever history it destroyed, left history in the gap, and was alive with the spirit of the deeds done midst its fashioning. The result of all this was often a building in which the many changes, though harsh and visible enough, were, by their very contrast, interesting and instructive and could by no possibility mislead. But those who make the changes wrought in our day under the name of Restoration, while professing to bring back a building to the best time of its history, have no guide but each his own individual whim to point out to them what is admirable and what contemptible; while the very nature of their task compels them to destroy something and to supply the gap by imagining what the earlier builders should or might have done. . . .

It is sad to say, that in this manner most of the bigger Minsters, and a vast number of more humble buildings, both in England and on the Continent, have been dealt with by men of talent often, and worthy of better employment, but deaf to the claims of poetry and history in the highest sense of the words.

For what is left we plead before our architects themselves, before the official guardians of buildings, and before the public generally, and we pray them to remember how much is gone of the religion, thought and manners of time past, never by almost universal consent, to be Restored; and to consider whether it be possible to Restore those buildings, the living spirit of which, it cannot be too often repeated, was an inseparable part of that religion and thought, and those past manners. . . . If, for the rest, it be asked us to specify what kind of amount of art, style, or other interest in a building, makes it worth protecting, we answer, anything which can be looked on as artistic, picturesque, historical, antique, or substantial: any work in short, over which educated, artistic people would think it worthwhile to argue at all. . . . we plead, and call upon those who have to deal with them to put Protection in the place of Restoration, to stave off decay by daily care, to prop a perilous wall or mend a leaky roof by such means as are obviously meant for support or covering, and show no pretence of other art, and otherwise to resist all tampering with either the fabric or ornament of the building as it stands; if it has become inconvenient for its present use, to raise another building rather than alter or enlarge the old one; in fine to treat our ancient buildings as monuments of a bygone art, created by bygone manners, that modern art cannot meddle with without destroying. . . .

22 JUNE 1877

To the Dean and Chapter of Canterbury Cathedral   The Society for the Protection of Ancient Buildings has heard with regret that it is the intention of the Dean & Chapter of Canterbury Cathedral, to remove from the Choir the ancient stalls which form such an interesting feature of the building. The Society feels it its duty to protest against such a course of action, which it considers injurious to the history, & art of the country. The Society begs to point out that this woodwork is remarkable for its intrinsic beauty, and although of comparatively late date, is a noble example of the art of its period, & in no way interferes with but rather adds to the Architectural Effect of the building. It is stated that these stalls conceal portions of more ancient work, part of the fittings of Prior Eastry, but as the work of that eminent architect is left in a very fragmentary condition, & any restoration must be, on the whole, conjectural as to design, and modern, as to workmanship, the Society feels that it would be a loss rather than a gain, to remove for the purpose of such restoration, a beautiful & untouched work of a former age. . . .

QUEEN SQUARE, 10 JULY 1877

To John Ruskin   We all think it might do good to distribute a leaflet with a reprint of your words on restoration in the Seven Lamps [*The Seven Lamps of Architecture* (1849)], will you allow me to do so? They are so good and so completely settle the whole matter that I feel ashamed at having to say anything else about it, as if the idea was an original one of mine, or any body's else but yours; but I suppose it is of service, or may be, for different people to say the same thing.

QUEEN SQUARE, 15 APRIL 1878

To the Editor, The Times   The question asked by Lord Houghton in the House of Lords on Thursday elicited from the Bishop of London an acknowledgement that the scheme proposed some few years back for the wholesale removal of the City churches is continuing its destructive course unimpeded. Four more churches are to be sacrificed to the Mammon-worship and want of taste of this great city. Last year witnessed the destruction of the fine church of St. Michael's, Queenhithe, and All Hallows, Bread-street, which bore upon its walls the inscription stating that Milton had been baptized there. St. Dion's Backchurch, a remarkable building by Wren, is now in course of destruction, while within the last ten years the beautiful church of St. Antholia, with its charming spire, and the skilfully designed little church of St. Mildred, in the Poultry, All Hallows, Staining (except its tower), St. James's, Duke-place, St. Bennet, Gracechurch, with its picturesque steeple, the tower and vestibule of All Hallows-the-Great, Thames-street, have all disappeared. Those for the removal of which a Commission has been now issued are as follows: – St. Margaret Pattens, Roodlane; St. George, Botolph-lane; St. Matthew, Friday-street; and St. Mildred, Bread-street, all works of Wren, and two of them – St. Mildred, Bread-street, and St. Margaret Pattens – possessing spires of singularly original and beautiful design. It must not be supposed that these are the only churches which are in danger, but their proposed destruction serves to show the fate which sooner or later is in store for the whole of Wren's churches in this city, unless Englishmen can be awakened, and by strong and earnest protest show the ecclesiastical authorities that they will not tamely submit to this outrageous and monstrous barbarity.

From an art point of view the loss of these buildings will be irreparable, for Wren's churches form a distinct link in the history of the ecclesiastical art of this country.

Many persons suppose that by preserving St. Paul's Cathedral, that architect's great masterpiece, enough will be left to illustrate his views upon ecclesiastical architecture, but this is far from being the case. For, grand as St. Paul's undoubtedly is, it is only one of a class of buildings common enough on the Continent – imitations of St. Peter's, Rome. In fact, St. Paul's can scarcely be looked upon as an English design, but, rather, as an English rendering of the great Italian original, whereas the City churches are examples of purely English renaissance architecture as applied to ecclesiastical purposes, and illustrate a style of architecture peculiar not only to this country but even to this city, and when they are destroyed the peculiar phase of architecture which they exhibit will have ceased to exist, and nothing will be left to record it. . . . One great merit which they possess is shown by the fact that, although they are diminutive in point of size, scarcely any one of them being about 80 ft. long, they possess a dignity of proportion, a masterly treatment as to scale, which renders them far more imposing than many buildings double and treble their dimensions; the relation which they bear to each other and to the great Cathedral which they surround, enhancing by their thin taper spires the importance of the majestic dome, and relieving the dulness and monotony of the general sky line of the City, all serve as unanswerable arguments for their preservation. . . .

31 OCT. 1879

To the Editor, The Daily News   I have just received information, on the accuracy of which I can rely, that the restoration of the west front of St. Mark's at Venice, which has long been vaguely threatened, is to be taken in hand at once. . . . The fate of such a building seems to me a subject important enough to warrant me in asking you to grant me space to make an appeal to your readers to consider what a disaster is threatened hereby to art and culture in general. Though this marvel of art and treasure of history has suffered some disgraces, chiefly in the base mosaics that have supplanted the earlier ones, it is in the main in a genuine and untouched state, and to the eye of anyone not an expert in building looks safe enough from anything but malice or ignorance. But anyhow, if it be in any way unstable, it

ST. MARK'S, VENICE, IN THE RAIN, 1846

is impossible to believe that a very moderate exercise of engineering skill would not make it as sound as any building of its age can be. Whatever pretexts may be put forward, therefore, the proposal to rebuild it can only come from those that suppose that they can renew and better (by imitation) the workmanship of its details, hitherto supposed to be unrivalled; by those that think that there is nothing distinctive between the thoughts, and expression of the thoughts, of the men of the twelfth and of the nineteenth century; by those that prefer gilding, glitter, and blankness, to the solemnity of tone, and the incident that hundreds of years of wind and weather have given to the marble, always beautiful, but from the first meant to grow more beautiful by the lapse of time; in short, those only can think the 'restoration' of St. Mark's possible who neither know nor care that it has now become a work of art, a monument of history, and a piece of nature. . . .

10 JUNE 1890

To Georgiana
. . . The next outing was an Anti-Scrape one to Lincoln. That was exceedingly delightful to me. The town has a terrible blot on it, a great factory for machines down by the river, which seem to take a pleasure in smoking; indeed I suppose its masters are practically the masters of the whole town. However, that is the worst of it: there is a longish, oldish street on the flat, and at the end of it a beautiful gate across, now the Guildhall, and it rises steeper and steeper till before you come to the close you almost have to crawl, and most of the way the leaden roof of the minster is the horizon; the houses mostly oldish red brick and pantiles. There is another most beautiful gate into the close, over which show the different planes of the minster most wonderfully. The whole place is chock full of history: there is the work of the first Norman bishop, Remigius, who strangely enough moved his see there from Dorchester on the Thames, so well known to me. The rest (and almost all) is in gradated periods of Early Pointed; outside one may perhaps find faults with parts, especially the East Front (only I had a pleasing feeling that I was not responsible for them). But when we got inside all criticism fell, and one felt – well, quite happy – and as if one never wanted to go away again. I had seen it all more than twenty years ago, but somehow was much more impressed this time: the church is not high inside, though it is long and broad, but its great quality is a kind of careful delicacy of beauty, that no other English minster that I have seen comes up to: in short a miracle of art, that nowhere misses its intention . . .

In the thick of poetry, blue-vats and business

Morris began to produce printed textiles in the early 1870s, working with Thomas Clarkson, of Bannister Hall Print Works near Preston in Lancashire. He was far from satisfied, however, with the chemical dyes that were used by commercial printers at the time, and in 1875 he began his long collaboration and friendship with Thomas Wardle, of Leek, Staffordshire. The Wardle family were silk dyers; George Wardle had become business manager of the Firm in 1870, following the death of

Warington Taylor, and he introduced Morris to his brother. The correspondence demonstrates Morris's tenacity and his refusal to make do with the second rate; for within a generation the use of chemicals had destroyed the art of vegetable dyeing, and Morris set himself to rediscover the ancient recipes and traditions, plying Wardle with old herbals, and himself experimenting with the dye vats at Queen Square.

Morris needed to expand the Firm's production at this time, not only because the move to Queen Square provided him with workshop space, but also because his inherited income was dwindling. His decision to take over the running of the Firm, which coincided with this need to earn more, obviously caused problems with some of the original partners, and widened the rift with Rossetti.

This, then, was one of the most productive periods of Morris's career – for, as well as his involvement with politics and design, he was also writing poetry, and beginning to translate the Icelandic sagas.

'RUPES TOPSEIA', 1875

QUEEN SQUARE, 22 OCT. 1873

To Louisa Baldwin
. . . I am wanting to settle down now into a really industrious man: for I do not mean to go to Iceland again if I can help it, and it is strange what a hole in my life that determination has made. . . . I am going to take to drawing from models again, for my soul's health chiefly, for little hope can I ever have to do anything

serious in the thing. It must be six years now since I made a habit of drawing and I never, if you can understand that, had the *painter's memory* which makes it easy to put down on paper what you think you see; nor indeed can I see any scene within a frame as it were round it, though in my own way I can realize things vividly enough to myself – I am also getting old, hard on 40 Louie, – so add all things together, and if I can tell you in six months time that I have been persevering in my drawing I give you leave therewith to praise my patience, though I can scarcely hope it will come to that . . .

To Dante Gabriel Rossetti Thanks for letter: I have no objections to make, but we must settle how the thing can be done, as the money must be vested in trustees.

For the rest, your views of the meeting I think are not likely to be correct in any one point (except that Marshall will certainly be drunk) for I don't think *he* will venture to face the indignant members, I will tell you why tomorrow, which will be worth at least one grin to you, I flatter myself: Webb Ned & Faulkner have all promised to come; and though Brown refuses, I have asked Watts to attend (which he has promised to do) so as to report what we have to say to Brown. In short I consider it an important meeting, even if Brown don't come & Watts said he would press him to do so. I expect to see Watts today, & he *may* bring me news of Browns being a little more reasonable though I confess I don't expect it. . . .

QUEEN SQUARE, 25 MAR. 1875

To Louisa Baldwin It was very kind of you and I thank you very much for remembering me and my birthday: I have been a happy man with my friends; nor do I think as far as my constant affection & good wishes are concerned that I have done otherwise than to deserve the goodhap. I am in my second half of my life now, which is likely to be a busy time with me, I hope till the very end: a time not lacking content too I fancy: I must needs call myself a happy man on the whole: and I do verily think I have gone over every possible misfortune in my own mind, & concluded that I can bear it if it should come . . .

QUEEN SQUARE, 25 MAR. 1875

To his mother . . . I have been working very hard lately, & have been much bothered by this law business the past 6 weeks: my recalcitrant partners have behaved so badly that I felt half inclined more than once to throw the whole affair into Chancery: but law is too ticklish a matter for one to throw one's whole chances for a livelihood into it: and I think I have done the best I could after all: though 'tis a deal of money to pay for shear nothing, and I doubt if their claims would have been recognized in the Court of Chancery . . .

QUEEN SQUARE, 27 MAY 1875

To Charles Fairfax Murray . . . I am up to the neck in turning out designs for papers chintzes and carpets and trying to get the manufacturers to do them . . .

124

17 JULY 1875

To his mother . . . On Monday I am going down to Staffordshire on manufacturing business & shall have to be at work there all the week . . .

LEEK (23 JULY 1875)

To Janey It seems to be quite settled now that I can't get back till this day week: I really can't come away without having come here for nothing, not that I haven't got on fairly well, but I must see something more of results – The copper pots in the dye-houses full of bright colours where they are dyeing silks look rather exciting: but alas! they are mostly aniline. Our own establishment is very small but I daresay will for sometime to come turn out more goods by a great deal than we shall sell. The country is certainly very pretty, a land of hillocks and little valleys, all curiously shaped. The last few days have been really beautiful except for a heavy shower just now . . .

WILLIAM MORRIS AND ROSALIND
HOWARD

LEEK, 30 JULY 1875

To Rosalind Francis Howard . . . I have been learning several interesting things here, and love art and manufactures, & hate commerce and moneymaking more than ever. I look forward to talking the whole matter over with you: though I daresay we will differ on a point or two.

QUEEN SQUARE, 3 AUG. 1875

To Thomas Wardle My bundle of fents [samples] were very much admired by my artistic friends, and almost all of them seem good in colour when they come among our things here: the only draw-back to my satisfaction is the Prussian blue, which is a terrible dissappointment: all the more as one of the blues and one of the greens were among the best

125

of the colours, and I had picked them out for orders at once: *but* they wash worse than Clarkson's blues; in fact worse than any I have ever seen and it would be useless for us to sell them in their present state: this is wholly a surprise to me as Hayworths washed pretty well, and we should have been contented with them in that condition: I enclose samples of Kay's and Hayworth's prussian's washed in *exactly the same way*: so you see it can be done: I beg to assure that I am quite vexed for the trouble that this will give you, but you must not be too downhearted about it for the madders are really very good colours, and the yellows seem to wash pretty well. So we shall have some 12 & 15 fents to print from.

My explanation of the affair is this: Hayworth was a steam-colour printer & knew nothing about madder; Kay is a madder-printer & knows nothing about steam colours. The last part of the sentence I will stick to till Kay produces a Prussian blue that will wash as well as 810, and you may tell him so. I blame myself for not making him soap some of the blue and green fents while I was there but you know I had troubles enough on hand.

What are we to do? First, can Kay be driven to make his blues as fast as Hayworth's? Second when can we have our indigo vats? We must give up blues and greens till one or both of these things is accomplished.

Meantime I need not say we must get on as fast as possible with the madders & yellows, additional orders for which I send down today. . . .

QUEEN SQUARE, AUG. 1875

. . . I have been looking about for a Gerard [*Herball* or *Generall Historie of Plants*, 1597] for you, but have not met with a good one yet, but suppose I shall soon. Meanwhile I have sent you a copy of Philemon Hollands Pliny [*Natural Historie of the World*]: a most curious book in itself and the translation a model of English: altogether one of the most amusing books in the world to my mind. . . .

QUEEN SQUARE, 21 OCT. 1875

To Aglaia Coronio   Thank you for your note, & 'kind enquiries': I am exceedingly well and in good spirits, & shall be very glad to see you when you come back. We have got a few pieces of printed cloths here, and they are hung up in the big room, where they look so beautiful (really) that I feel inclined to sit and stare at them all day; which however I am far from doing as I am working hard: I don't suppose we shall get many people to buy them however; which will be a pity as we shall be obliged in that case to give up the manufacture. Item, we have got a pattern of woollen cloth that pleases me hugely, though I don't know if it would please you, for it looks quite like a medieval manufacture.

All this keeps me busy and amuses me very much, so that I consider myself a lucky man, among so many people who seem to find it hard to be amused.

QUEEN SQUARE, 28 OCT. 1875

To Thomas Wardle   The two pieces of green for 967 are very bad indeed: they are not in the least to pattern, & I doubt if they will be of any use at all to us.

Meantime we are starving for the want of completion of really useful orders. What are we [to] do? the worst of the fents sent before for this colour was better than this: I confess I am quite discouraged: Kay does not seem to be able to do anything, even the simplest matching, and it is all a matter of luck how things go: I believe he thinks we can't do without him, and that he can do anything he pleases: I don't suggest sacking him at once in the face of all the present orders, but we can't be forever under his hippopotamus thumb –.

We want stock sadly: we have sold the best of the little lot we had. . . .

'THE BARD AND PETTY TRADESMAN'

QUEEN SQUARE, 2 NOV. 1875

Thanks for your long letter: after what you say about the matching I will leave the matter in your hands, except for one thing, which has happened more than once and of which this morning gives us a strong example: to wit: Kay sends us a few days ago a fent of which No. 1 is a strip as a pattern of how the finished good will be, when printed from the colour he has mixed for them: this morning the finished goods are to hand, and No. 2 is a strip from them: now I can't believe that Kay has not altered the colour between the time that we said 'go on', and the printing of the pieces . . . The fact is the man's mind is a perfect muddle: however no doubt we must put up with him at present, at least while we get cloths we can use . . .

QUEEN SQUARE, 5 NOV. 1875

Thanks for your letter. 1st as to prices, we must assume that matter settled for the 6 months; I must accept your offer about the 4 block carnation or I shan't be able to sell it at all.

I must say though, that I hope at the 6 months end you will find it possible to reduce the prices considerably: if not I can't help seeing that the sale is likely to be very limited. The prices are more than double Clarkson's for block-printed cloths, and *his* prices are I am sure from the way we began business with him calculated above the usual scale . . .

. . . For the men, I am surprised that such creatures can exist – which I think I have said

PAGES FROM THE MERTON
ABBEY DYE BOOK, 1882–91

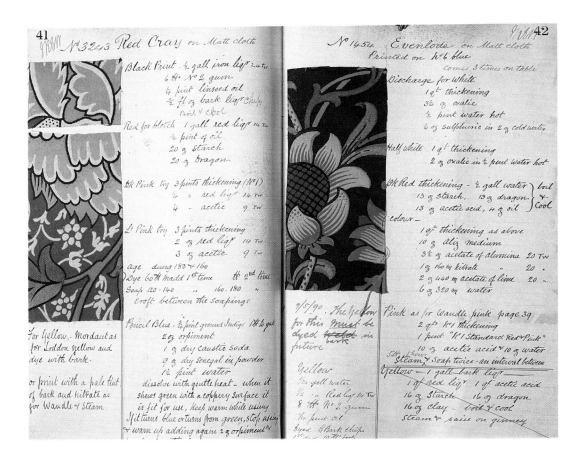

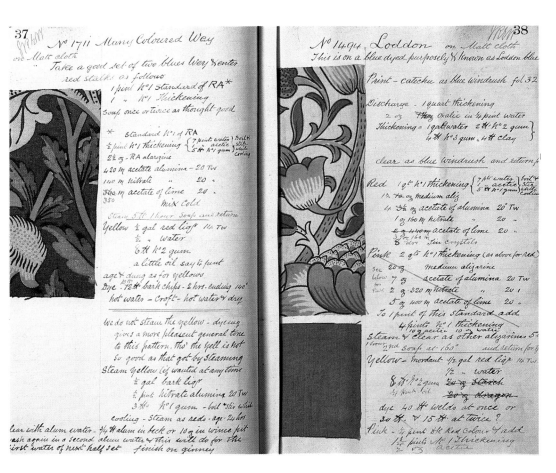

before: – but, seriously, you seem in your letter to admit all that I have ever charged them with, i.e. disregarding orders: if they had other qualities to make up for it this might be put up with, but as it is I believe they will beat you even in trying to carry out these first few orders of ours. One thing I must remind you of, that their obstinate refusal to make an ordinary match of *their own* patterns almost entirely nullifies whatever advantage may be derived from my artistic knowledge & taste, *on which the whole of my business depends*; however, the subject of these monsters of idiocy is a dismal one & I will say no more than to beg you to impress on them the necessity of following out their instructions to the letter *whatever may be the results*. The new patterns I am about are not more difficult it seems to me than the old ones; but I may be obliged to hold them back on the score of expense . . .

QUEEN SQUARE, 16 NOV. 1875

Thanks for your letter: I don't want to think I under estimate your difficulties, many of which no doubt I know nothing about: I want to point out to you however that our *essential* requirements as to colours are but few: the variety of the orders is a great deal due to the uncertainties of matching: If the matter were got to a matter of routine we should want these *standards* of colour and *no more* for the steam-colour styles . . .

. . . I send you a rag from the bed which heard my first squeak: my mother says it is about 6 years older than myself: I suppose it to be all indigo & madder except the yellow: the indigo is very nice and bright; whether it is dip blue or china I don't know but it has certainly been blocked in some way; I have a yard or two in my museum, if you wish to see more of it . . .

QUEEN SQUARE, 23 NOV. 1875

I proceed to answer both your letters before I begin work this morning. 1st woad ['the Northern hemisphere's version of the Eastern indigo'] Couldn't anything be learned in France about this subject, where they seem to have used it later than we at all events? The indigo on my natal print is *certainly* blocked in, as you would see if you had a bigger piece: I suspect Kay don't know as much on the subject as the present writer, who now sendeth you a piece of cloth pencilled on (nothing will do but the chewed willow twig) by his own hands: it is very easy to lay on, but I fancy we shall not easily get it brighter than the enclosed specimen: I have a block, now in the cutter's hands very elaborate as to print, but very simple as to blotch on which we might at least try this blue: please however to refrain your natural grin of triumph when I mention that it is no use trying it on *un*bleached cloth.

Of course you would have children for the pencilling: our boys at 5/6 a week would be quite up to it. I should have thought (with deference) that we scarcely wanted more printers . . .

. . . I don't think you should look forward to our *ever* using a machine. As to the mercantile branch, that is quite out of *our* way: but I see no reason why *you* should not try it, if you think it would pay; and I should be happy to help in the designing way . . .

. . . I must beg you to consider our many difficulties in the way of getting anything good done, and not to leave us in the lurch and to receive the assurance again from me, if you need it, that I fully understand the value of working in open day with an honourable & sympathetic person like yourself and am quite prepared to support you by any means in my power.

I am also as you must know most deeply impressed with the importance of having all our dyes the soundest & best that can be, and am prepared to give up all that part of my business which depends on textiles if I fail in getting them so: however I don't in the least see why I should talk to you about failing which is after all impossible, as I have no doubt you feel yourself . . .

QUEEN SQUARE, MONDAY (MAR. 1876?)

To Aglaia Coronio

. . . as to what I am doing, I am drawing patterns so fast that last night I dreamed I had to draw a sausage; somehow I had to eat it first, which made me anxious about my digestion: however I have just done quite a pretty pattern for printed work. . . .

QUEEN SQUARE, 8 MAR. 1876

To Janey

. . . The Embroidery ladies gave me such a turn of it this morning I thought I should have been both walked and talked off my legs. I am withal in the thick of poetry, blue-vats and business. I finished by the way, by buying *both* those pieces of embroidery for £160: I think I have as good as sold one of them: but of course I shall keep them until you come back . . .

LEEK, 28 MAR. 1876

To Aglaia Coronio

. . . I am working in Mr. Wardle's dye-house in sabots and blouse pretty much all day long: I am dyeing yellows and reds: the yellows are very easy to get, and so are a lot of shades of salmon and flesh-colour and buff and orange; my chief difficulty is in getting a deep blood red, but I hope to succeed before I come away: I have not got the proper indigo vat for wool, but I can dye blues in the cotton vat and get lovely greens with that and the bright yellow that weld gives.

This morning I assisted at the dyeing of 20 lbs of silk (for our damask) in the blue vat; it was very exciting, as the thing is quite unused now, and we ran a good chance of spoiling the silk. There were four dyers and Mr Wardle at work, and myself as dyers' mate: the men were encouraged with beer and to it they went, and pretty it was to see the silk coming green out of the vat and gradually turning blue; we succeeded very well as far as we can tell at present; the oldest of the workmen, an old fellow of seventy, remembers silk being dyed so, long ago. The vat you must know, is a formidible-looking thing, 9 ft deep and about 6 ft square: and is sunk into the earth right up to the top. To-morrow I am going to Nottingham to see wool dyed blue in the woad vat, as it is called; on Friday Mr Wardle is going to dye 80 lbs. more silk for us, and I am going to dye about 20 lbs in madder for my deep red. With all this I shall be very glad indeed to be home again, as you may well imagine.

PHOTOGRAPH OF MORRIS, DATE UNKNOWN

To Thomas Wardle   . . . As to going on with the enterprise of the wool-dyeing, I am determined to do so in some way or other; because so much of my work depends on the solving of the difficulty, that no amount money could compensate me for the dissappointment if I had to give it up: at the same time I don't suppose the dyeing of our wools will ever be a profitable business to anyone, and no doubt it will be a troublesome one: so I for my part I wish you to consider if it is worth your while to undertake it: which you must necessarily do for the pleasure of the thing than for commercial reasons: I think it only fair to put this before you, as the calico-printing has been such a troublesome affair . . . my only other plan would be to try to get a couple of men and do it in London, out Hammersmith way, as well I could; and I have no doubt I should flounder about finely in the blunder-sea . . .

. . . We have just got in two trial pieces of our three-ply carpet woven of my dyeing-attempts, they both look very well, but as one of them is vat-blue we must leave that for the present: but the red one we want got into the loom as soon as may be, so I want to know if you can undertake 400-weight of wool for it; all cochineal and madder, and how long it would be in dyeing from the day you got the wool to hand: I will send you patterns of everything with notes as to how I got the colours, and as to which variations from pattern would be harmful & which would be of little importance . . .

. . . I am very wishful to see a good fent of the honeysuckle pattern: also the green & blue carnation is much wanted . . .

. . . I have got a copy of Hellot (Paris 1750) who is only about wool dyeing: he is very minute about the management of the vats, and I think might be of some use in that quarter, as he wanted to do with his vats as we do, viz make all the shades of blue to be used: he has an interesting chap: on Kermes [an insect dye], which he praises as the best and fastest of colours, as fast as madder: but I am afraid our chances of meeting with that drug are but slight.

I was amused to hear how you had kept your council about Kays departure when you were up here: I hope all will go well with the new man: I am waiting anxiously for your plant getting advanced enough to give us the dip blue: as well as the wool & silk dyeing . . .

PS Today we have had bad accounts of another set of silk curtains of our selling: green this time, dyed at Lyons: as far as dyers are concerned I wish the days of Colbert [minister in reign of Louis XIV] back again: it was red last time and Tours.

QUEEN SQUARE, 31 OCT. 1876

. . . Walnuts – I have been able to get very few of them, don't you think you might get some up there as you will be later than us: remembering all you said about the difficulty of saddening [toning down colours] silk, I cannot help thinking they would be very useful to us. I shall make you laugh when I tell you that on Saturday I tried another new dyeing material poplar-twigs to wit: I was promised a yellow out of them, but managed nothing nearer to it than a pleasant brown shading off to Nankin or buff colour . . .

Af. Mar. [African Marigold] looks very fine, but you must not forget to print the *heads*

A PAGE FROM THOMAS WARDLE'S DYE BOOK, 1875

with a light shade of it: you remember there is a separate block for that purpose . . . By the way shall we dispense with the ceremony of 'Mistering' one another, in future, if you don't think it rude.

QUEEN SQUARE, 17 NOV. 1876

. . . I was at Kelmscott the other day in that beautiful cold weather and betwixt the fishing, I cut a handful of poplar twigs & boiled them, and dyed a lock of wool a very good yellow: this would be useful if fast, for the wool was *un*mordanted . . .

QUEEN SQUARE (17–30 NOV. 1876?)

. . . The difficulties of your carrying on a private manufactory for us, a business which *must* in the nature of things be rather what is called today an art rather than a manufacture, I feel, as I have always have felt, to be immense: . . . I mean that I can never be contented with getting anything short of the best, and that I shall always go on trying to improve our goods in all ways, and should consider anything that was only tolerable as a ladder to mount up to the next stage – that is, in fact, my life . . .

LICHFIELD, 4 FEB. 1877

To Georgiana

. . . Leek, Monday . . . I have been dyeing in *her* [the blue-vat] all the afternoon, and my hands are a woeful spectacle in consequence . . . I lost my temper in the dyehouse for the first time this afternoon: they had been very trying: but I wish I hadn't been such a fool; perhaps they will turn me out tomorrow morning, or put me in the blue-vat.

LEEK, 7 FEB. 1877

To Janey

. . . I cannot get back till next Saturday, which will make two days more than the fortnight, but even then I shall have left a great deal unsettled . . . Please I shall want a bath when I come home: you may imagine that I shall not be very presentable as to colour: I have been dyeing in the blue-vat today; we had to work it at 130° and a hot work it was, as you must keep the goods clean under the surface of the bath. It will be a difficult matter to arrange dyeing the shades: our vat is too strong at present for quite light shades: I have been red-dyeing also, but have not tackled the greens and yellows yet: I must try to do something in them before I go: I set myself too much work to do: that is a fact. . . .

HORRINGTON HOUSE, 25 MAR. 1877

To Thomas Wardle

. . . I have been thinking much since I saw you about beginning manufacturing in the small way as soon as I can: my trouble is that for the thing to be done satisfactorily it must be done in London (since I live there).

I have asked my Kidderminster friend to see about a carpet weaver for me there; and besides I very much want to set up a loom for *brocade* weaving: would it be possible to get a Frenchman over from Lyons under the present circumstances of the trade there? I would give a year's engagement certain to a real clever fellow who would do what I wanted him to do: I am dazzled at the prospect of the splendid work we might turn out in that time.

The single piece of Snake-head that came up last week was very good: I don't know that I don't like it best of all that we have done.

I am studying birds now to see if I can't get some of them into my next design.

We shall open our shop [at 264 Oxford St] just after Easter I imagine, if that matters.

QUEEN SQUARE, 10 APRIL 1877

. . . Thanks also for good wishes about the shop: I think it will answer though I can't say I am much excited about it, as I should be if it were a shed with half a dozen looms in it.

. . . The tapestry is a bright dream indeed: but it must wait until I can get my carpets going: though I have had it in my head lately, because there is a great sale going on in Paris of some of the finest ever turned out: much too splendid for any but the biggest pots to buy . . . Meantime much may be done in carpets: I saw yesterday a piece of *ancient* Persian time of Shah Abbas (our Elizabeth's time) that fairly threw me on my back: I had no idea such wonders could be done in carpets . . .

QUEEN SQUARE, 29 JUNE 1877

To George Howard . . . Our Froggy weaver is over here and many a time in the day have I cause to curse that basest of jargons so grossly misnamed the Frankish or French tongue.

QUEEN SQUARE, 28 JULY 1877

To Thomas Wardle I write in real tribulation about the silk-warp Bazin is idle, now; though in very truth he has been ill & in St. Thomas Hospital meanwhile: we must really manage to begin at something. or I swear I will bolt . . .

QUEEN SQUARE, 24 OCT. 1877

Thanks for sending the things, but I'm afraid I must trouble you further, for Maquer, & my sabots & apron carelessly left behind in my retreat from Leek. Please thank Mrs Wardle for sending me the spectacles . . .

. . . The *Widow Guelph* [Queen Victoria] has been enticing our customers from us & has got an order for tapestry that ought to have been ours; so much for Kings & Scoundrels: you will have to join me in the end crying death to the aristocrats! – or at all events to their coats.

QUEEN SQUARE, 14 NOV. 1877

Like you I shall probably find one letter's space not enough for going into the whole matter of the tapestry, but I will begin: Let's clear off what you say about the possibility of establishing a non-artistic manufactory; you could do it of course; 'tis only a matter of money and trouble: but cui bono? it would not amuse you . . . and would I am sure *not* pay commercially – a *cheap* new article at once showy and ugly if advertised with humbug enough will sell of course: but an expensive article, even with ugliness to recommend it – I don't think anything under a Duke could sell it: however, as to the commercial element of this part of the scheme, 'tis not my affair, but on the art-side you must remember that, as nothing is so beautiful as fine tapestry, nothing is so ugly and base as bad; eg. the Gobelins or the present Aubusson work: also tapestry is not fit for anything but figure-work . . . 'tis the only way of making a web into a picture: now there is only one man at present living, (as far as I know) who can give you pictures at once good enough and suitable for tapestry – to wit Burne-Jones – the exception . . . would be the making of leaf & flower-pieces (greeneries, des Verdures) which would be generally used to eke out a set of figure-pieces: these would be within the compass of people, work-folk, who could not touch the figure-work; it would only be by doing these that you could cheapen the work at all.

The qualification for a person who could do successful figure-work would be these:

1. General feeling for art, especially for its decorative side.
2. He must be a good colourist.
3. He must be able to draw well; ie he must be able to draw the human figure, especially hands and feet.
4. Of course he must know how to use the stitch of the work.

. . . I suspect you scarcely understand what a difficult matter it is to translate a painter's design into material: I have been at it 16 years now, & have never quite succeeded. In spite of all these difficulties if in anyway I can help you I will: only you must fully understand that I intend setting up a frame and working at it myself, and I should bargain for my being taught by you what is teachable: also I see no difficulty in your doing greeneries & what patterns turned out desirable, & I would make myself responsible for the design of such matters. With all this, I have no doubt that we shall both lose money over the work: you don't know how precious little people care for such things. . . .

KELMSCOTT MANOR, 3 OCT. 1879

To Georgiana   Somehow I feel as if there must soon be an end for me of playing at living in the country: a town-bird I am, a master-artisan, if I may claim that latter dignity.

KELMSCOTT MANOR, 13 OCT. 1879

As to poetry, I don't know, and I don't know. The verse would come easy enough if only I had a subject which would fill my heart and mind: but to write verse for the sake of writing it is a crime in a man of my years and experience . . .

I have seen a many wonders, and have good memory for them; and in spite of all grumblings have a hope that civilized people will grow weary of their worst follies and try to live a less muddled and unreasonable life; not of course that we will see much of that change in the remnant that is left of our days.

AUTUMN 1879

Lord bless us how nice it will be when I can get back to my little patterns and dyeing, and the dear warp and weft at Hammersmith.

WORKING DRAWING FOR JASMINE WALLPAPER, *c*. 1872

JASMINE WALLPAPER, 1872

UTRECHT VELVETS, *c.* 1871

DESIGN FOR TULIP AND WILLOW, 1873

TULIP AND WILLOW PRINTED COTTON, 1873

LOVE IS ENOUGH, PROOF, *c.* 1871

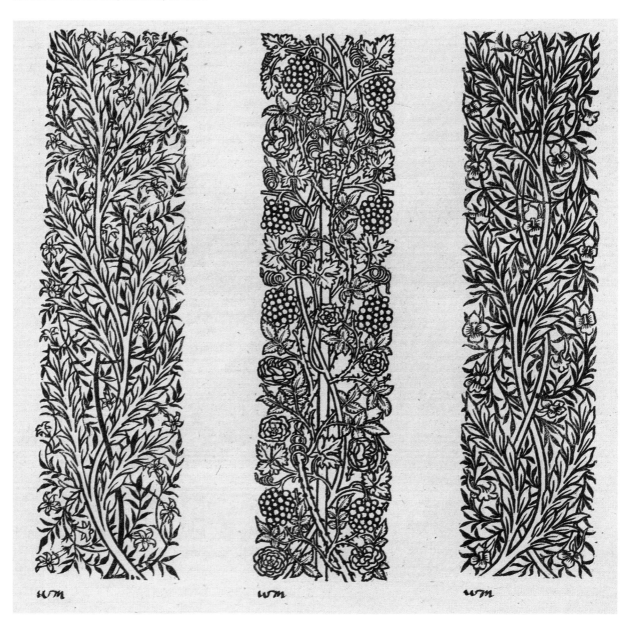

HORACE *ODES*, MANUSCRIPT, 1874

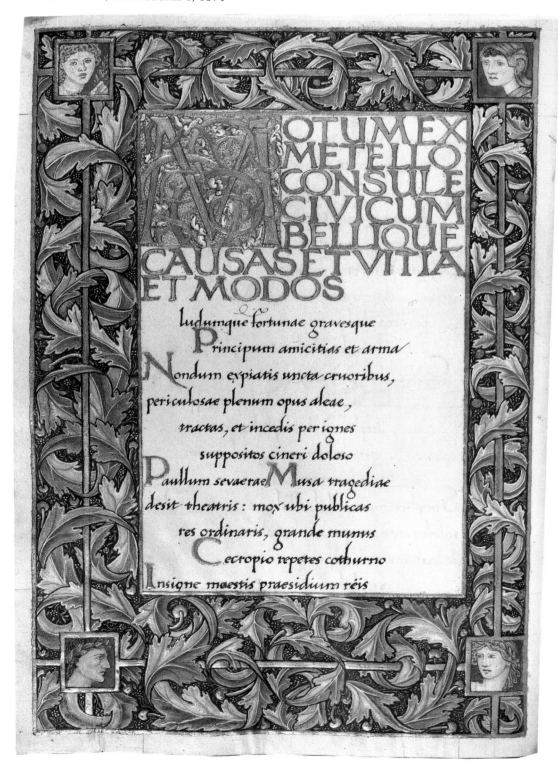

THE RUBAIYAT OF OMAR KHAYYAM, MANUSCRIPT, 1872

ICELANDIC STORIES, MANUSCRIPT, *c.* 1873

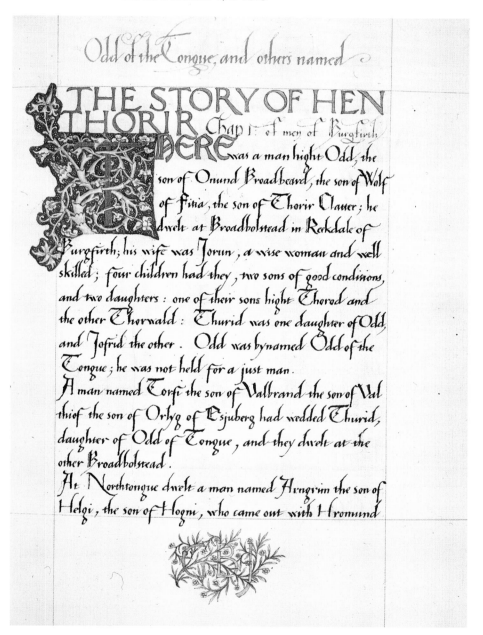

Odd of the Tongue, and others named

THE STORY OF HEN THORIR

Chap I: of men of Burgfirth

HERE was a man hight Odd, the son of Onund Broadbeard, the son of Wolf of Fitia, the son of Thorir Clatter; he dwelt at Broadbolstead in Reekdale of Burgfirth; his wife was Jorun, a wise woman and well skilled; four children had they, two sons of good conditions, and two daughters: one of their sons hight Thorod and the other Thorwald: Thurid was one daughter of Odd, and Jofrid the other. Odd was bynamed Odd of the Tongue; he was not held for a just man.

A man named Torfi the son of Valbrand the son of Valthiof the son of Orlyg of Esjuberg had wedded Thurid, daughter of Odd of Tongue, and they dwelt at the other Broadbolstead.

At Northtongue dwelt a man named Arngrim the son of Helgi, the son of Hogni, who came out with Hromund

WILLOW WALLPAPER, 1874

LINOLEUM, 1875

DESIGN FOR BAYLEAF EMBROIDERY, DATE UNKNOWN

THE FLOWERPOT EMBROIDERY, *c.* 1876

NORTH BEDROOM, STANDEN

POWDERED WALLPAPER, 1874

DESIGN FOR MINSTREL
TILES, *c.* 1872

MINSTREL TILES,
c. 1872−4

DESIGNS FOR OXFORD UNION CEILING, 1874–5

'LARKSPUR' BEDROOM, STANDEN

LARKSPUR WALLPAPER, 1872

DESIGN FOR ACANTHUS WALLPAPER, 1875

ACANTHUS WALLPAPER, 1875

WOODBLOCK FOR TULIP, 1875   DESIGN FOR TULIP, 1875

TULIP PRINTED COTTON, 1875

INDIAN DIAPER PRINTED COTTON, 1875

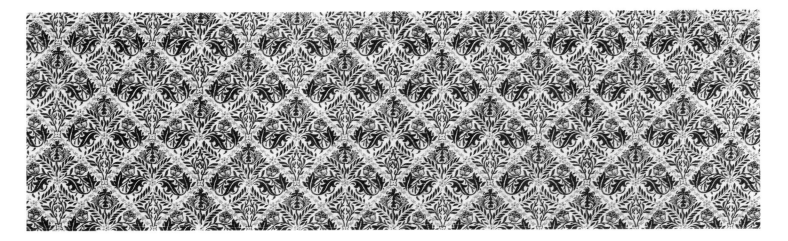

DESIGN FOR CHRYSANTHEMUM WALLPAPER, 1876

BILLIARD ROOM, WIGHTWICK MANOR, STAFFORDSHIRE

PIMPERNEL WALLPAPER, 1875

DESIGN FOR IRIS, 1876

IRIS PRINTED COTTON, 1876

DESIGN FOR FLORAL PATTERN TILES, 1876

FLORAL PATTERN TILES, 1876

DESIGN FOR BLUEBELL OR COLUMBINE PRINTED COTTON, 1876

BLUEBELL OR COLUMBINE PRINTED COTTON, 1876

DESIGN FOR HONEYCOMB, 1876

HONEYCOMB WOVEN WOOL, 1876

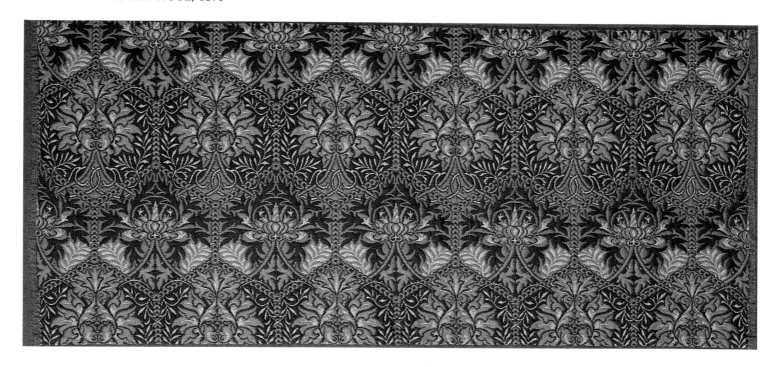

SNAKEHEAD PRINTED COTTON, 1876

SNAKEHEAD PRINTED COTTON, 1876

DESIGN FOR HONEYSUCKLE PRINTED COTTON, 1874

HONEYSUCKLE PRINTED COTTON, 1876

DESIGN FOR HONEYSUCKLE WALLPAPER, 1879—81

HONEYSUCKLE WALLPAPER, 1883

DESIGN FOR AFRICAN MARIGOLD, 1876

AFRICAN MARIGOLD PRINTED COTTON, 1876

POMEGRANATE PRINTED COTTON, 1877

LITTLE CHINTZ FABRIC, 1876

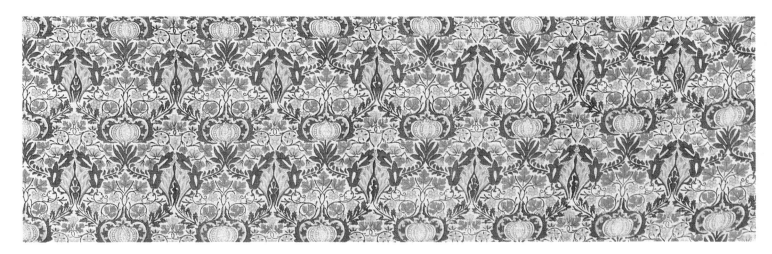

ARTICHOKE EMBROIDERED PANEL, 1877

ACANTHUS HANGING, *c.* 1880

DESIGN FOR BIRD, 1878

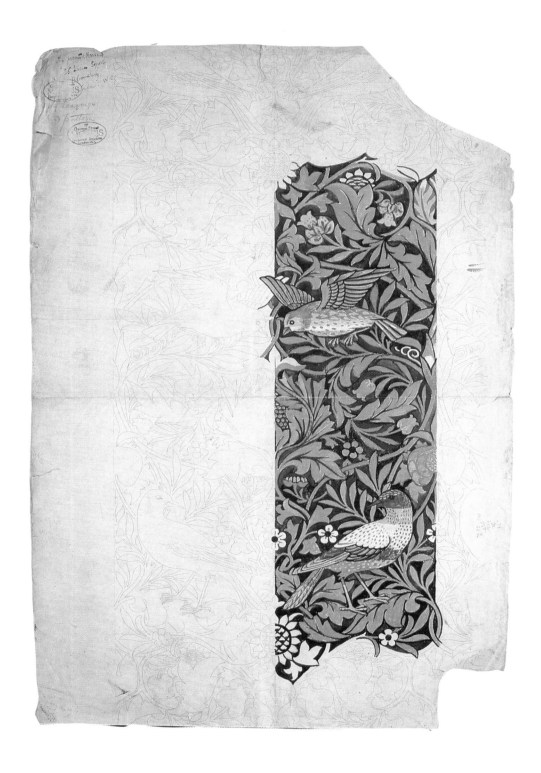

BIRD WOVEN WOOL DOUBLE CLOTH, 1878

DESIGN FOR BIRD AND PALM TREE, DATE UNKNOWN

PEACOCK AND DRAGON WOVEN WOOL, 1878

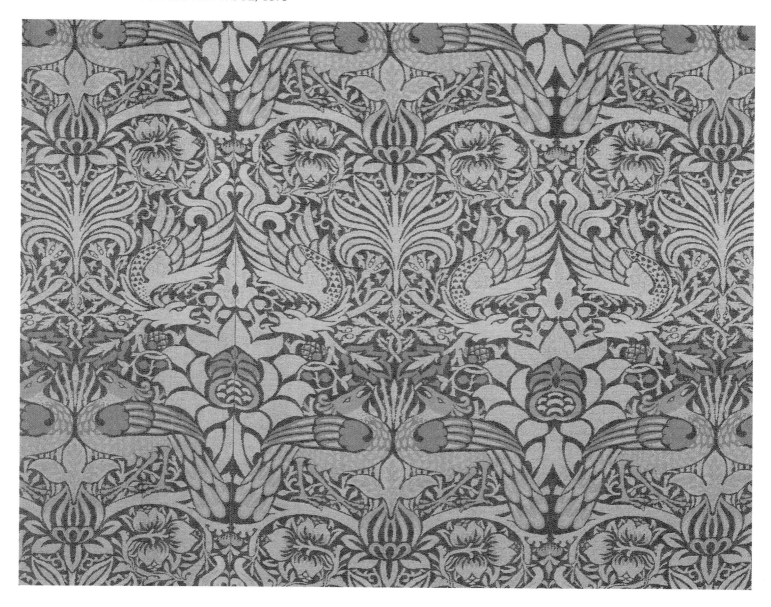

DESIGN FOR BIRD AND VINE WOVEN FABRIC, 1878

CABBAGE AND VINE (VINE AND ACANTHUS) TAPESTRY, 1879

WORKING DRAWING FOR DOVE
AND ROSE, 1879

DRAWING ROOM, WIGHTWICK MANOR, STAFFORDSHIRE

DRAWING FOR PINK AND POPPY (ALSO KNOWN AS POPPY), DATE UNKNOWN

DESIGN FOR ACANTHUS, 1879

FLOWER GARDEN WOVEN SILK, 1879

ACANTHUS WOVEN SILK, 1879

DESIGN FOR SUNFLOWER WALLPAPER, 1879

SUNFLOWER WALLPAPER, 1879

DESIGN AND SOCIALISM

Merton Abbey

In June 1881 Morris moved his workshops from Queen Square to Merton Abbey in Surrey. The premises he found there, on a seven-acre site, had been established as a silk-weaving factory by the Huguenots in the early eighteenth century, and more recently had been used for printing cheap table-cloths. The river Wandle – 'even now but a little spoilt', according to Mackail in 1899, ran through the grounds 'turning a water wheel and supplying water of the special quality required for madder dyeing.' The workshops consisted of long wooden two-storeyed sheds, red-tiled and weather-boarded, and there was an orchard and vegetable garden as well as meadows on the site. There was also a house, where the boys employed in the workshops were lodged. Morris was able to extend and control his production at Merton; he could now dye and print his textiles, and he at last fulfilled his 'bright dream' of designing and making tapestries, as well as rugs and carpets.

A circular issued when the Merton Abbey workshops were fully operational catalogues the work that could be done there:

1. *Painted glass windows.*
2. *Arras tapestry woven in the high-warp loom.*
3. *Carpets.*
4. *Embroidery.*
5. *Tiles.*
6. *Furniture.*
7. *General house decorations.*
8. *Printed cotton goods.*
9. *Paper hangings.*
10. *Figured woven stuffs.*
11. *Furniture velvets and cloths.*
12. *Upholstery.*

It was at this time, however, that Morris began to refuse glass commissions for old churches, the ideals of the Society for the Protection of Ancient Buildings preventing him from undertaking even this form of 'restoration'. He writes in the circular:

'We are prepared as heretofore to give estimates for windows in churches and other buildings, except in the case of such as can be considered monuments of Ancient Art, *the glazing of which we can not conscientiously undertake, as our doing so would seem to sanction the disastrous practice of so-called Restoration.'*

Morris also kept a diary in 1881 and the entries indicate not only how hard he worked, but also how determined he was at this time to master the technique as well as the art of tapestry weaving:

March 12 . . . up at 7.30, about four hours tapestry.

March 19 . . . up at 6$\frac{1}{2}$, four hours tapestry.

April ?? . . . up at 6, two hours tapestry.

April ?? . . . up at 5.30, three hours tapestry.

May 12. Up late. Worked on paper hanging in the morning. In afternoon to Office of Works about St. James. To S.P.A.B. dined Grange. 4 [hours] at Howard's carpet. Wind E. in morning: seemed to change to S. in evening: bright in morning: warm all day but cloudy in afternoon bright night.

May 20 . . . Up at 5: 3$\frac{1}{2}$ hrs tapestry. To Grange. To Queen Square: The green for Peacock all wrong. Did day books and Friday [signing cheques, etc.] besides seeing to this took away model of G.H. carpet ['Nawarth', for George Howard] from K. Meeting St Mark's Committee. Dined A. Ionides. Wind W.S.W. very fine, bright day. Cool in evening.

THE POND AT MERTON ABBEY, WATERCOLOUR

19 MAR. 1881

To Janey   Wardle and Webb are gone today to have a look at those premises at Merton . . . There are decided advantages about the . . . place: first, it would scarcely take me longer to get there from Hammersmith than it now does to Queen Square: next it is already a print-works (for those hideous red & green table-cloths and so forth) so that the plant would be really useful to us: 3rd the buildings are not bad: 4th the rent (£200) can be managed, if we can settle all that, as at present what is offered for sale is the tail-end of a lease and the plant. 5th the water is abundant and good. 6th though the suburb as such is woeful beyond conception, yet the place itself is even very pretty: Summa I think it will come to taking it, if we can get it on fair terms . . .

From Mackail

. . . It is a lovely day here, though it was dark and thick in town; but I cannot get about the works, for the gout has made another grab at me . . . I have ordered the cab to be here about 6 to take me back to Hammersmith, and I have plenty of small designing work to do meantime. As to our printing we are really not quite straight yet: I am quite ashamed of it: however they are doing Brother Rabbit successfully, and the Anemone will go on now, and when we are once out of this difficulty, I really think that we shall have seen the worst of it. Item, we are going to get our wheel set straight during the Christmas holidays, so as not to stop work; the poor critter ['creature' = wheel] wants it very badly, for every now and then when there is not much water on, it really seems as if he stopped to think, like a lazy boy turning a grindstone. . . .

KELMSCOTT HOUSE, 14 MAR. 1883

To Jenny

. . . we are not getting on so fast as we ought with the printing at Merton: I was away for a fortnight with gout, & Wardle was away more than usual: the colour mixer Kenyon is a good fellow, but rather a muddler, & often in order to be sure that the thing is properly done either I or Wardle have to stand over him all the time: this is specially the case with the madder dyeing which we are now on . . .

HIGH WARP TAPESTRY
WEAVING, MERTON ABBEY,
c. 1890

. . . I was a great deal at Merton last week, though I didn't sleep there, anxiously superintending the first printing of the Strawberry Thief which I think we shall manage this time . . .

. . . I have been to Merton to-day, and after a morning shower it turned out so beautiful! I had a pleasant day on the whole things are going on fairly: the marsh marigolds are all out and are splendid; one clump by the tail-side is a picture . . .

To Andreas Scheu
. . . If you want to know anything more in detail about dyeing, or any other matter of my work, I shall be happy to tell you, or to show you what we do at Merton Abbey, where I am both a dyer and a cotton-printer: only you understand we only use the old methods that obtained before the apotheosis of shoddy, and the free exchange of adulterated wares which Gladstone praised so at Kirkwall the other day . . .

To John Ruskin
. . . We *paint* on glass; first the lines of draperies, features & the like, with an opaque colour which when the glass is held up to the light is simply so much obscurity; with thinner washes and scumbles of the same colour we shade objects as much as we deem necessary, but always using this shading to explain form, and not as shadow proper.

2nd. Finding that it was difficult to get a flesh-coloured glass with tone enough for the flesh of figures, we use thin washes of a reddish enamel colour to stain white glass for flesh-colour & sometimes, though rarely, for other pale orange tints: N.B. this part of our practice is the only point in which we differ from that of the mediaeval glass-painters.

3rd. We use a yellow stain on white glass (or on blue to make greens): this is chiefly done by means of silver, is quite transparent & forms part of the glass after firing; it may therefore be considered rather a diffusion of the colour in the glass than a painting on it.

The body of the glass is of two kinds, first what is technically called pot-metal, in which the colouring matter is fused with the glass, & is essentially part of it: and 2ndly what is called flashed glass, in which a white body is covered with a coloured skin: this is done by the workman taking on the end of his hollow rod first a large lump of white metal, then a small dip of coloured metal; he then trundles the lot, making a disk like a small piece of crown glass. This kind of glass however is not much used except for the red coloured by copper called technically 'ruby glass', this owing to its make is often curiously and beautifully striped & waved: this glass is, I must tell you, perilous to fire the painted colours upon, as the kiln generally changes it more or less, sometimes darkening it almost to blackness, sometimes carrying the colour away: to avoid this risk we are sometimes obliged to paint the necessary lines on a piece of thin white glass & lead up the two together: this, which is called plating I have sometimes done with two pieces of coloured glass, to get some peculiar tint: one must be careful not to overdo the process however, or you will get a piece of glass at once cumbrous & liable to accident.

I should mention that all the glass is very thick: and that in some of the pot-metals, notably the blues, the difference between one part of a sheet and another is very great. This variety is very useful to us in getting a jewel-like quality which is the chief charm of painted glass – when we *can* get it. You will understand that we rely almost entirely for our colour on the actual *colour of the glass*; and the more the design will enable us to break up the pieces, and the more mosaic-like it is, the better we like it. . . .

PRINTING CHINTZES, MERTON ABBEY, *c.* 1890

1 JUNE 1884

To Georgiana

. . . Some of those who work for me share in the profits formally: I suppose I made the last year or two about £1800, Wardle about £1200, the Smiths about £600 each, Debny and West £400. All these share directly in the profits: Kenyon, the colour mixer, & Goodacre, the foreman dyer, have also a kind of bonus on the amount of goods turned out: the rest either work as day-workers, or are paid by the piece, mostly the latter: in both cases they get more than the market price of their labour: two or three people about the place are no use to the business and are kept on on the live-and-let-live principle, not a bad one I think as things go, in spite of the Charity Organization Society.

The business has of course a certain capital to work on, about £1500, which is very little for the turn-over of goods: this is nominally mine, but of course I can't touch it as long as the business is going, and if the business were wound up it is doubtful if it would realize more than enough to pay the debts, since goods always sell for less than their value at forced sales. . . .

Hopes and fears for Art

Morris gave his first lecture, 'The Decorative Arts' (later called 'The Lesser Arts') to the Trades Guild of Learning in December 1877. He took great pains over its preparation, for although he was so prolific and fluent a writer of letters, poems and romances, preparing lectures did not come easily to him. ('I know what I want to say,' he wrote of a later lecture to Georgiana, 'but the cursed words go to water between my fingers.') Nevertheless Morris was in great demand as a speaker: 'The Decorative Arts' was the first of many lectures that he gave in the later years of his life.

In all these lectures, Morris relates his ideals for art and craftsmanship to social conditions, and to his personal and evolving social concerns. In some, however, he writes very specifically about what he describes as 'the manner of work' – the nature of design and the design process.

Morris published several of these lectures in his own lifetime: Hopes and Fears for Art *was published in 1882, and* Signs of Change *in 1888. A further collection,* Architecture, Industry and Wealth, *was published in 1902. He was also contributing to* The Commonweal *and* Justice, *as well as to Arts and Crafts publications.*

From 'The Lesser Arts' [lecture, 1877] . . . Our subject is that great body of art, by means of which men have at all times more or less striven to beautify the familiar matters of everyday life: a wide subject, a great industry; both a great part of the history of the world and a most helpful instrument to the study of that history.

A very great industry indeed, comprising the crafts of house-building, painting, joinery and carpentry, smiths' work, pottery and glass-making, weaving, and many others: a body of art most important to the public in general, but still more so to us handicraftsmen; since there is scarce anything that they use, and that we fashion, but it has always been thought to be unfinished till it has had some touch or other of decoration about it. . . . We have got so used to this ornament, that we look upon it as if it had grown of itself, and see it no more than the mosses on the dry sticks with which we light our fires. So much the worse! for there *is* the decoration, or some pretence of it, and it has, or ought to have, a use and a meaning. For . . . everything made by man's hands has a form, which must be either beautiful or ugly; beautiful if it is in accord with Nature, and helps her; ugly if it is discordant with Nature, and thwarts her; it cannot be indifferent . . . Now it is one of the chief uses of decoration, the chief part of its alliance with nature, that it has to sharpen our dulled senses in this matter: for this end are those wonders of intricate patterns interwoven, those strange forms invented, which men have so long delighted in: forms and intricacies that do not necessarily imitate nature, but in which the hand of the craftsman is guided to work in the way that she does, till the web, the cup, or the knife, look as natural, nay as lovely, as the green field, the river bank, or the mountain flint.

To give people pleasure in the things they must perforce *use*, that is one great office of decoration; to give people pleasure in the things they must perforce *make*, that is the other use of it . . .

. . . These arts . . . are the sweeteners of human labour, both to the handicraftsman, whose life is spent in working in them, and to people in general who are influenced by the sight of them at every turn of the day's work: they make our toil happy, our rest fruitful . . .

. . . when we can get beyond [the] smoky world, there, out in the country we may still see the works of our fathers yet alive amidst the very nature they were wrought into, and of which they are so completely a part: for there indeed if anywhere, in the English country, in the days when people cared about such things, was there a full sympathy between the works of man and the land they were made for: – the land is a little land; too much shut up within the narrow seas, as it seems, to have much space for swelling into hugeness: there are no great wastes overwhelming in their dreariness, no great solitudes of forests, no terrible untrodden mountain-walls: all is measured, mingled, varied, gliding easily one thing into another: little rivers, little plains, swelling, speedily changing uplands, all beset with handsome orderly trees; little hills, little mountains, netted over with the walls of sheep-walks: all is little; yet not foolish and blank, but serious rather, and abundant of meaning for such as choose to seek it: it is neither prison nor palace, but a decent home . . .

. . . For as was the land, such was the art of it while folk yet troubled themselves about such things; it strove little to impress people either by pomp or ingenuity: not unseldom it fell into commonplace, rarely it rose into majesty; yet was it never oppressive, never a slave's nightmare nor an insolent boast: and at its best it had an inventiveness, an

THE STAINED GLASS STUDIO, MERTON ABBEY, *c.* 1890

individuality that grander styles have never overpassed: its best too, and that was in its very heart, was given as freely to the yeoman's house, and the humble village church, as to the lord's palace or the mighty cathedral: never coarse, though often rude enough, sweet, natural and unaffected, an art of peasants rather than of merchant-princes or courtiers, it must be a hard heart, I think, that does not love it . . . it clung fast to the life of the people, and still lived among the cottagers and yeomen . . . while the big houses were being built 'French and fine': still lived also in many a quaint pattern of loom and printing-block, and embroiderer's needle, while overseas stupid pomp had extinguished all nature and freedom, and art was become, in France especially, the mere expression of that successful and exultant rascality, which in the flesh no long time afterwards went down into the pit for ever . . .

. . . nothing can be a work of art which is not useful; that is to say, which does not minister to the body when well under command of the mind, or which does not amuse, soothe, or elevate the mind in a healthy state. What tons upon tons of unutterable rubbish pretending to be works of art in some degree would this maxim clear out of our London houses, if it were understood and acted upon! . . . as a rule all the decoration (so called) . . . is there for the sake of show, not because anybody likes it. I repeat, this stupidity goes through all classes of society: the silk curtains in my Lord's drawing-room are no more a matter of art to him than the powder in his footman's hair; the kitchen in a country farmhouse is most commonly a pleasant and homelike place, the parlour dreary and useless.

. . . I do not want art for a few, any more than education for a few, or freedom for a few . . .

From 'The Art of the People' [lecture, 1879]   . . . History (so called) has remembered the kings and warriors, because they destroyed; Art has remembered the people, because they created . . .

. . . though many of us love architecture dearly, and believe that it helps the healthiness both of body and soul to live among beautiful things, we of the big towns are mostly compelled to live in houses which have become a by-word of contempt for their ugliness and inconvenience. The stream of civilisation is against us, and we cannot battle against it . . .

. . . That thing which I understand by real art is the expression by man of his pleasure in labour. I do not believe he can be happy in his labour without expressing that happiness; and especially is this so when he is at work at anything in which he specially excels . . .

. . . To plough the earth, to cast the net, to fold the flock – these, and such as these, which are rough occupations enough, and which carry with them many hardships, are good enough for the best of us, certain conditions of leisure, freedom, and due wages being granted. As to the bricklayer, the mason, and the like – these would be artists, and doing not only necessary, but beautiful, and therefore happy work, if art were anything like what it should be. No, it is not such labour as this which we need to do away with, but the toil which makes the thousand and one things which nobody wants, which are used merely as the counters for the competitive buying and selling, falsely called commerce . . .

ST. JAMES'S WOVEN SILK
DAMASK, 1881

. . . Meanwhile, if these hours be dark, as, indeed, in many ways they are, at least do not let us sit deedless, like fools and fine gentlemen, thinking the common toil not good enough for us, and beaten by the muddle; but rather let us work like good fellows trying by some dim candle-light to set our workshop ready against to-morrow's daylight – that to-morrow, when the civilised world, no longer greedy, strifeful, and destructive, shall have a new art, a glorious art, made by the people and for the people, as a happiness to the maker and the user.

STANMORE HALL, STANMORE, MIDDLESEX, *c.* 1891

From 'The Beauty of Life' [lecture, 1880] . . . whereas all works of craftsmanship were once beautiful, unwittingly or not, they are now divided into two kinds, works of art and non-works of art: now nothing made by man's hand can be indifferent: it must be either beautiful and elevating, or ugly and degrading; and those things that are without art are so aggressively . . .

. . . out of all despair sprang a new time of hope lighted by the torch of the French Revolution: and things that have languished with the languishing of art, rose afresh and surely heralded its new birth: in good earnest poetry was born again, and the English Language, which under the hands of sycophantic verse-makers had been reduced to a miserable jargon, whose meaning, if it have a meaning, cannot be made out without translation, flowed clear, pure, and simple, along with the music of Blake and Coleridge: take those names, the earliest in date among ourselves, as a type of the change that has happened in literature since the time of George II.

With that literature in which romance, that is to say humanity, was re-born, there sprang up also a feeling for the romance of external nature . . . joined with a longing to know something real of the lives of those who have gone before us; of these feelings united you will find the broadest expression in the pages of Walter Scott: it is curious . . . that the man who wrote the exquisite and wholly unfettered naturalism of the Heart of Midlothian, for instance, thought himself continually bound to seem to feel ashamed of, and to excuse himself for, his love of Gothic Architecture: he felt that it was romantic, and he knew that it gave him pleasure, but somehow he had not found out that it was art, having been taught in many ways that nothing can be art that was not done by a named man under academical rules . . .

. . . The lack of art, or rather the murder of art, that curses our streets from the sordidness of the surroundings of the lower classes, has its exact counterpart in the dullness and vulgarity of those of the middle classes, and the double-distilled dullness, and scarcely less vulgarity of those of the upper classes . . .

. . . how . . . can you really educate men who lead the life of machines, who only think for the few hours during which they are not at work, who in short spend almost their whole lives in doing work which is not proper for developing them body and mind in some worthy way? You cannot educate, you cannot civilise men, unless you can give them a share in art . . .

. . . I had thought that civilisation meant the attainment of peace and order and freedom, of goodwill between man and man, of the love of truth and the hatred of injustice . . . not more stuffed chairs and more cushions, and more carpets and gas, and more dainty meat and drink – and therewithal more and sharper differences between class and class . . .

. . . Perhaps it will not try your patience too much if I lay before you my idea of the fittings necessary to the sitting-room of a healthy person: a room, I mean, which he would not have to cook in much, or sleep in generally, or in which he would not have to do any very litter-making manual work.

First a book-case with a great many books in it: next a table that will keep steady when you write or work at it: then several chairs that you can move, and a bench that you can sit or lie upon: next a cupboard with drawers: next, unless either the book-case or the cupboard be very beautiful with painting or carving, you will want pictures or engravings, such as you can afford, only not stopgaps, but real works of art on the wall; or else the wall itself must be ornamented with some beautiful and restful pattern: we shall also want a vase or two to put flowers in, which latter you must have sometimes, especially if you live in a town. Then there will be the fireplace of course, which in our climate is bound to be the chief object in the room.

That is all we shall want, especially if the floor be good; if it be not, as, by the way, in a modern house it is pretty certain not to be, I admit that a small carpet which can be bundled out of the room in two minutes will be useful, and we must also take care that it is beautiful, or it will annoy us terribly . . .

. . . This simplicity you may make as costly as you please or can, on the other hand: you may hang your walls with tapestry instead of whitewash or paper; or you may cover them with mosaic, or have them frescoed by a great painter: all this is not luxury, if it be done for beauty's sake, and not for show: it does not break our golden rule: *Have nothing in your houses which you do not know to be useful or believe to be beautiful.*

. . . To have breasted the Spanish pikes at Leyden, to have drawn sword with Oliver: that may well seem to us at times amidst the tangles of to-day a happy fate: for a man to be able to say, I have lived like a fool, but now I will cast away fooling for an hour, and die like a man – there is something in that certainly: and yet 'tis clear that few men can be so lucky as to die for a cause, without having first of all lived for it. And as this is the most that can be asked from the greatest man that follows a cause, so it is the least that can be taken from the smallest.

. . . since we are servants of a Cause, hope must be ever with us, and sometimes perhaps it will so quicken our vision that it will outrun the slow lapse of time, and show us the victorious days when millions of those who now sit in darkness will be enlightened by an *Art made by the people and for the people, a joy to the maker and the user.*

HAMMERSMITH CLUB LECTURE
ANNOUNCEMENT, 1886

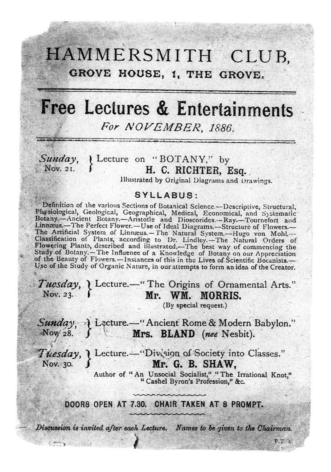

From 'The Lesser Arts of Life' [lecture 1882]   . . . I must needs think of furniture as two kinds, one part of it being chairs, dining and working tables, and the like, the necessary workaday furniture in short, which should, of course be well made and well proportioned, but simple to the last degree . . . But besides this type of furniture, there is the kind I should call state furniture, which I think is proper, even for a citizen: I mean sideboards, cabinets, and the like, which we have quite as much for beauties' sake as for use; we need not spare ornament on these, but may make them as elegant and elaborate as we can with carving, inlaying, or painting; these are the blossoms of the art of furniture . . .

From evidence given to the Royal Commission on Technical Instruction (1882)

. . . I think undoubtedly everybody ought to be taught to draw, just as much as everybody ought to be taught to read and write . . . It is a thing to be deprecated that there should be a class of mere artists who furnish designs ready-made to what you may call the technical designers. I think it is desirable that the artist and what is technically called the designer should practically be one . . . A designer ought to be able to weave himself. . . .

From The Clarion *[interview 1892]*

'. . . I have got to understand thoroughly the manner of work under which the Art of the Middle Ages was done, and that is the *only* manner of work which can turn out popular art, only to discover that it is impossible to work in that manner in this profit-grinding society . . . Except with a small part of the more artistic side of the work, I could not do anything (or at least but little) to give this pleasure to the workmen, because I should have had to change their method of work so utterly that I should have disqualified them from earning their living elsewhere . . .

'. . . I have tried to produce goods which are genuine as far as their mere substances are

BILL FROM MORRIS AND CO., 1887

concerned, and should have on that account the primary beauty in them which belongs to naturally treated substances; have tried, for instance to make woollen substances as woollen as possible, cotton as cotton as possible and so on; I have only used the dyes which are natural and simple . . .'

From 'Art and the Beauty of the Earth' [lecture, 1881]   . . . You who in these parts make such hard, smooth, well compacted, and enduring pottery understand well that you must give it other qualities besides those which make it fit for ordinary use. You must profess to make it beautiful as well as useful, and if you did not you would certainly lose your market . . .

. . . When men have given up the idea that the work of men's hands can ever be pleasurable to them, they must, as good men and true, do their utmost to reduce the work of the world to a minimum . . .

. . . Machines then. . . . I myself have boundless faith in their capacity. I believe machines can do everything, except make works of art . . .

. . . Hold fast to distinct form in art. Don't think too much of style, but set yourself to get out of you what you think beautiful, and express it, as cautiously as you please, but . . . quite distinctly, and without vagueness. Always think your design out in your head before you begin to get it on the paper. Don't begin by slobbering and messing about in the hope that something may come out of it. You must see it before you can draw it, whether the design be of your own invention or nature's. Remember always, form before colour, and outline, silhouette, before modelling; not because these latter are of less importance, but because they can't be right if the first are wrong . . .

. . . try to get the most out of your material, but always in such a way as honours it most. Not only should it be obvious what your material is, but something should be done with it which is specially natural to it, something that could not be done with any other. This is the very *raison d'être* of decorative art: to make stone look like ironwork, or wood like silk, or pottery like stone is the last resource of the decrepitude of art. Set yourselves as much as possible against all machine work (this to all men). But if you have to design for machine work, at least let your design show clearly what it is. Make it mechanical with a vengeance, at the same time as simple as possible. Don't try, for instance, to make a printed plate look like a hand-painted one: make it something which no one would try to do if he were painting by hand. . . .

From 'Textiles' [article, 1893]   . . . The noblest of the weaving arts is Tapestry, in which there is nothing mechanical: it may be looked upon as a mosaic of pieces of colour made up of dyed threads, and is capable of producing wall ornament of any degree of elaboration within the proper limits of duly considered decorative work.

As in all wall-decoration, the first thing to be considered in the designing of Tapestry is the force, purity, and elegance of the *silhouette* of the objects represented, and nothing vague or indeterminate is admissable . . . it also demands that crispness and abundance of beautiful detail which was especially characteristic of Mediaeval Art . . .

. . . Carpet-weaving is somewhat of the nature of Tapestry . . . it is also wholly unmechanical, but its use as a floor-cloth somewhat degrades it, especially in our northern or western countries, where people come out of the muddy streets into rooms without taking off their shoes . . .

. . . Owing to the comparative coarseness of the work, the designs should always be very elementary in form, and *suggestive* merely of forms of leafage, flowers, beasts and birds, etc. The soft gradations of tint to which Tapestry lends itself are unfit for Carpet-weaving; beauty and variety of colour must be attained by harmonious juxtaposition or tints, bounded by judiciously chosen outlines; and the pattern should lie absolutely flat upon the ground . . .

. . . I have been thinking only of the genuine or hand-made carpets. The mechanically-made carpets of to-day must be looked upon as makeshifts for cheapness' sake. . . . The velvet carpets need the same kind of design as to colour and quality as the real carpets; only, as the colours are necessarily limited in number, and the pattern must repeat at certain distances, the design should be simpler and smaller than in a real carpet. A Kidderminster carpet calls for a small design in which the different planes, or piles, as they are called, are well interlocked.

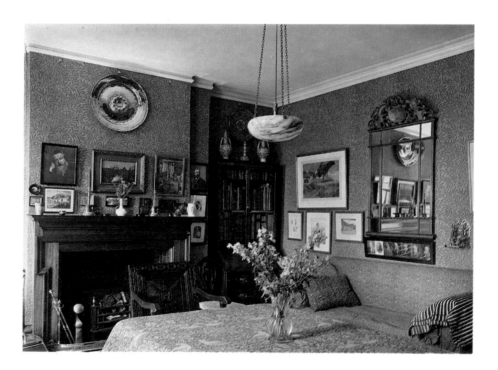

EMERY WALKER'S HOUSE, HAMMERSMITH TERRACE

Mechanical weaving has to repeat the pattern on the cloth within comparatively narrow limits; the number of colours also is limited in most cases to four or five. In most cloths so woven, therefore, the best plan seems to be to choose a pleasant ground colour and to superimpose a pattern mainly composed of either a lighter shade of that colour, or a colour in no very strong contrast to the ground; and then, if you are using several colours, to light up this general arrangement either with a more forcible outline, or by spots of a stronger colour carefully disposed . . . In any case, the patterned webs produced by mechanical weaving, if the ornament is to be effective and worth the doing, require that same Gothic crispness and clearness of detail which has been spoken of before: the geometrical structure of the pattern, which is a necessity in all recurring patterns, should be boldly insisted upon, so as to draw the eye from accidental figures, which the recurrence of the pattern is apt to produce.

The meaningless stripes and spots and other tormentings of the simple twill of the web, which are so common in the woven ornament of the eighteenth century and in our times should be carefully avoided: all these things are the last resource of a jaded invention and a contempt of the simple and fresh beauty that comes of a sympathetic *suggestion* of natural forms: if the pattern be vigorously and firmly drawn with a true feeling for the beauty of line and *silhouette*, the play of light and shade on the material of the simple twill will give all the necessary variety . . .

. . . The next method of ornamenting cloth is by painting it or printing on it with dyes. As to the painting of cloths with dyes by hand, which is no doubt a very old and widely practised art, it has now quite disappeared . . . and its place has been taken by printing by block or cylinder-machine. The remarks made on the design for mechanically woven cloths apply pretty much to these printed stuffs: only, in the first place, more play of delicate and pretty colour is possible, and more variety of colour also; and in the second, much more use can be made of hatching and dotting, which are obviously suitable to the method of block-printing. In the many-coloured printed cloths, frank red and blue are again the mainstays of the colour arrangement; these colours, softened by the paler shades of red, outlined with black and made more tender by the addition of yellow in small quantities, mostly forming part of brightish greens, make up the colouring of the old Persian prints, which carry the art as far as it can be carried . . .

. . . Last of the methods of ornamenting cloth comes Embroidery: of the design for which it must be said that one of its aims should be the exhibition of beautiful material. Furthermore, it is not worth doing unless it is either very copious and rich, or very delicate – or both. For such an art nothing patchy or scrappy, or half-starved, should be done . . . It may be well here to warn those occupied in Embroidery against the feeble imitations of Japanese art which are so disastrously common amongst us. The Japanese are admirable naturalists, wonderfully skilful draughtsmen, deft beyond all others in mere execution of whatever they take in hand; and also great masters of style within certain narrow limitations. But with all this, a Japanese design is absolutely worthless unless it is executed with Japanese skill. In truth, with all their brilliant qualities as handicraftsmen, which have so dazzled us, the Japanese have no architectural, and therefore no decorative, instinct. Their works of art are isolated and blankly individualistic, and . . . remain mere wonderful toys, things quite outside the pale of the evolution of art, which, I repeat, cannot be carried on without the architectural sense that connects it with the history of mankind . . .

. . . never forget the material you are working with, and try always to use it for what it can do best: if you feel yourself hampered with the material in which you are working, instead of being helped by it, you have so far not learned your business . . . The special limitations of the material should be a pleasure to you, not a hindrance: a designer, therefore, should always thoroughly understand the processes of the special manufacture of the material he is dealing with, or the result will be a mere *tour de force*. On the other hand, it is the pleasure in understanding the capabilities of a special material, and using them for suggesting (not imitating) natural beauty and incident, that gives the *raison d'être* of decorative art.

A river of fire

Morris joined the Democratic Federation (later Social Democratic Federation) in 1883, thus formally allying himself with the emerging Socialist party. He contributed articles and poems (including Chants for Socialists) *to the SDF's magazine* Justice, *and began to lecture and write about socialism. Differences of opinion with his colleagues in the SDF, however, led him to resign from that organization, and to become a founder member of the Socialist League. He edited (and largely financed) its journal,* The Commonweal, *in which* The Pilgrims of Hope *(1885–1886),* A Dream of John Ball *(1888) and* News from Nowhere *(1891) were first published.*

In 1890 he was forced to resign from the Socialist League, and in the last years of his life any formal allegiances he had were with the Hammersmith Socialist Society.

KELMSCOTT HOUSE, 22 JUNE 1883

To C.E. Maurice   . . . A word about the Democratic Federation: as far as I know it is the only active Socialist organization in England; under the above mentioned circumstances therefore I found myself bound to join it, although I had heard beforehand (to speak plainly) that it was a sort of Tory drag to take the scent off the fox. From all I can hear I believe that to be a calumny: or, to speak English, one of those curious lies for which no one seems responsible, but which stick very tight to the object they are thrown at. However that may be, I cannot see how a Society which has declared openly for Socialism, including Land Nationalization, can serve the Tory cause, whatever the Tory intention may be: for the rest, from what I can see from their proceedings the Executive seem to me to mean work; and if their opinions hurt the Liberal party (where is it by the way?) it is the fault of the Liberal party for allowing itself to stiffen into Whiggery or practical Toryism, as it seems to me it is fast doing . . .

KELMSCOTT HOUSE, 1 JULY 1883

. . . I do not believe in the world being saved by any system, – I only assert the necessity of attacking systems grown corrupt, and no longer leading anywhither: that to my mind is the case with the present system of capital and labour: as all my lectures assert, I have personally been gradually driven to the conclusion that art has been handcuffed by it, and will die out of civilization if the system lasts . . .

1 JUNE 1884

To Georgiana . . . And now I want to explain once more this: that if these were ordinary times of peace I might be contented amidst my discontent, to settle down into an ascetic hermit of a hanger-on; such a man as I should respect even now: but I don't see the peace or feel it; on the contrary fate, or what not has forced me to feel war, and lays hands on me as a recruit: therefore do I find it not only lawful to my conscience but even compulsory on it to do what in times of peace would not perhaps be lawful, and certainly would not be compulsory: if I am wrong, I am wrong and there is an end of it: I can't expect pardon or consideration of anyone – and shan't ask it. . . .

KELMSCOTT HOUSE, 24 JULY 1884

To Robert Thompson . . . we cannot turn our people back into Catholic English peasants and Guild craftsmen, or into heathen Norse bonders, much as may be said for such conditions of life . . .

. . . Whatever Socialism may lead to, our aim, to be always steadily kept in view, is, to obtain for the whole people, duly organized, the possession and control of all the means of production and exchange, destroying at the same time all national rivalries. . . .

ADVERTISING LABEL FOR *THE COMMONWEAL*, c. 1888

From 'How I became a Socialist' [article, 1894] . . . what I mean by Socialism is a condition of society in which there should be neither rich nor poor, neither master nor master's man, neither idle nor overworked, neither brain-sick brain workers, nor heart-sick hand workers, in a word, in which all men would be living in equality of condition, and would manage their affairs unwastefully, and with the full consciousness that harm to one would mean harm to all — the realization at last of the meaning of the word COMMONWEALTH.

MEMBERS OF THE SOCIALIST LEAGUE, HAMMERSMITH

    Now this view of Socialism which I hold to-day, and hope to die holding, is what I began with; I had no transitional period, unless you may call such a brief period of political radicalism during which I saw my ideal clear enough, but had no hope of any realization of it. That came to an end some months before I joined the (then) Democratic Federation, and the meaning of my joining that body was that I had conceived a hope of the realization of my ideal. If you ask me how much of a hope, or what I thought we Socialists then living and working would accomplish towards it, or when there would be effected any change in the face of society, I must say, I do not know. I can only say that I did not measure my hope, nor the joy that it brought me at the time. For the rest, when I took that step I was blankly ignorant of economics; I had never so much as opened Adam Smith, or heard of Ricardo, or of Karl Marx. . . . Well, having joined a Socialist body (for the Federation soon became definitely Socialist), I put some conscience into trying to learn the economical side of Socialism, and even tackled Marx, though I must confess that, whereas I thoroughly enjoyed the historical part of *Capital*, I suffered agonies of confusion of the brain over reading the pure economics of that great work. Anyhow, I read what I could, and will hope that some information stuck to me from my reading . . . Such finish to what of education in practical Socialism as I am capable of I received afterwards from some of my Anarchist friends, from whom I learned, quite against their intention, that Anarchism was impossible . . .

But in this telling how I fell into *practical* Socialism I have begun, as I perceive, in the middle, for in my position of a well-to-do man, not suffering from the disabilities which oppress a working man at every step, I feel that I might never have been drawn into the practical side of the question if an ideal had not forced me to seek towards it. . . . nor when I had become conscious of the wrongs of society as it now is, and the oppression of poor people, could I have ever believed in the possibility of a *partial* setting right of those wrongs. In other words, I could never have been such a fool as to believe in the happy and 'respectable' poor. . . .

Before the uprising of *modern* Socialism almost all intelligent people either were, or professed themselves to be, quite contented with the civilization of this century. . . . To be short, this was the *Whig* frame of mind, natural to the modern prosperous middle-class men, who, in fact, as far as mechanical progress is concerned, have nothing to ask for, if only Socialism would leave them alone to enjoy their plentiful style.

. . . there were a few who were in open rebellion against the said Whiggery – a few, say two, Carlyle and Ruskin. The latter, before my days of practical Socialism, was my master towards the ideal aforesaid, and, looking backward, I cannot help saying, by the way, how deadly dull the world would have been twenty years ago but for Ruskin! . . . Apart from the desire to produce beautiful things, the leading passion of my life has been and is hatred of modern civilization. What shall I say of it now, when the words are put into my mouth, my hope of its destruction – what shall I say of its supplanting by Socialism?

What shall I say concerning its mastery of and its waste of mechanical power, its commonwealth so poor, its enemies of the commonwealth so rich, its stupendous organization – for the misery of life! Its contempt of simple pleasures which everyone could enjoy but for its folly? Its eyeless vulgarity which has destroyed art, the one certain solace of labour? All this I felt then as now, but I did not know why it was so. The hope of the past times was gone, the struggles of mankind for many ages had produced nothing but this sordid, aimless, ugly confusion; the immediate future seemed to me likely to intensify all the present evils by sweeping away the last survivals of the days before the dull squalor of civilization had settled down on the world. (This was a bad look-out indeed, and, if I may mention myself as a personality and not as a mere type, especially so to a man of my disposition, careless of metaphysics and religion, as well as of scientific analysis, but with a deep love of the earth and the life on it, and a passion for the history of the past of mankind. Think of it!) Was it all to end in a counting-house on the top of a cinder-heap, with Podsnap's drawing-room in the offing, and a Whig committee dealing out champagne to the rich and margarine to the poor in such convenient proportions as would make all men contented together, though the pleasure of the eyes was gone from the world, and the place of Homer was to be taken by Huxley? . . . So there I was in for a fine pessimistic end of life, if it had not somehow dawned on me that amidst all this filth of civilization the seeds of a great change, what we others call Social-Revolution, were beginning to germinate. The whole face of things was changed to me by that discovery, and all I had to do then in order to become a Socialist was to hook myself on to the practical movement, which, as before said, I have tried to do as well as I could.

To sum up, then the study of history and the love and practice of art forced me into a hatred of the civilization which, if things were to stop as they are, would turn history into inconsequent nonsense, and make art a collection of the curiosities of the past, which would have no serious relation to the life of the present. . . .

From 'The Prospects of Architecture' [article, 1881]

. . . We of the English middle classes are the most powerful body of men that the world has yet seen . . . and yet when we come to look the matter in the face, we cannot fail to see that even for us with all our strength it will be a hard matter to bring about that birth of the new art: for between us and what is to be, if art is not to perish utterly, there is something alive and devouring; something as it were a river of fire that will put all that tries to swim across it to a hard proof indeed, and scare from the plunge every soul that is not made fearless by desire of truth and insight of the happy days to come beyond . . .

From Chants for Socialists

from 'All for the Cause'

There midst the world new-builded shall our earthly deeds abide,
Though our names be all forgotten, and the tale of how we died.

Life and death then, who shall heed it, what we gain or what we lose?
Fair flies life amid the struggle, and the Cause for each shall choose.

Hear a word, a word in season, for the day is drawing nigh,
When the Cause shall call upon us, some to live, and some to die!

from 'A Death Song'

What cometh here from west to east awending?
And who are these, the marchers stern and slow?
We bear the message that the rich are sending
Aback to those who bade them wake and know.
Not one, not one, nor thousands must they slay,
But one and all if they would dusk the day.

We asked them for a life of toilsome earning,
They bade us bide their leisure for our bread;
We craved to speak to tell our woeful learning;
We come back speechless, bearing back our dead.
Not one, not one, nor thousands must they slay,
But one and all if they would dusk the day.

They will not learn; they have no ears to hearken.
They turn their faces from the eyes of fate;
Their gay-lit halls shut out the skies that darken.
But, lo! This dead man knocking at the gate.
Not one, not one, nor thousands must they slay,
But one and all if they would dusk the day.

From The Pilgrims of Hope

from 'The Message of the March Wind'

Hark! the March wind again of a people is telling;
Of the life that they live there, so haggard and grim,
That if we and our love amidst them had been dwelling
My fondness had faltered, thy beauty grown dim.

This land we have loved in our love and our leisure
For them hangs in heaven, high out of their reach;
The wide hills o'er the sea-plain for them have no pleasure,
The grey homes of their fathers no story to teach.

The singers have sung and the builders have builded,
The painters have fashioned their tales of delight;
For what and for whom hath the world's book been gilded,
When all is for these but the blackness of night?

from 'The Story's Ending'

And I cling to a love of the past and the love of the day to be,
And the present, it is but the building of the man to be strong in me.

From 'How we live and how we might live' *[article, 1887]*

. . . the Indian or Javanese craftsman may no longer ply his craft leisurely, working a few hours a day, in producing a maze of strange beauty on a piece of cloth: a steam engine is set a-going in Manchester, and that victory over nature and a thousand stubborn difficulties is used for the base work of producing a sort of plaster china-clay and shoddy, and the Asiatic worker, if he is not starved to death outright, as plentifully happens, is driven himself into a factory to lower the wages of his Manchester brother worker, and nothing of character is left him except, most like, an accumulation of fear and hatred of that to him most unaccountable evil, his English master. The South Sea Islander must leave his canoe-carving, his sweet rest, and his graceful dances, and become the slave of a slave: trousers, shoddy, rum, missionary, and fatal disease – he must swallow all this civilization in a lump, and neither himself nor we can help him now till social order displaces the hideous tyranny of gambling that has ruined him.

Let those be the types of consumer: but now for the producer; I mean the real producer, the worker; how does this scramble for the plunder of the market affect him? . . . when the glut comes in that market . . . what happens to this army, every private in which has been depending on the steady demand in that market, and acting, as he could not choose but act, as if it were to go on for ever? You know very well what happens to these men: the factory door is shut on them; on a very large part of them often, and at the best on the reserve army of labour, so busily employed in the time of the inflation. . . . But what we don't know, or don't choose to know, is that this reserve army of labour is an absolute necessity for commercial war; if *our* manufacturers had not got these poor devils whom they could draft on to their machines when the demand swelled, other manufacturers, in France or Germany, or America, would step in and take the market from them . . .

. . . I have spoken of machinery being used freely for releasing people from the more mechanical and repulsive part of necessary labour; and I know that to some cultivated people, people of the artistic turn of mind, machinery is particularly distasteful, and they will be apt to say you will never get your surroundings pleasant so long as you are surrounded by machinery. I don't quite admit that; it is the allowing machines to be our masters and not our servants that so injures the beauty of life nowadays . . .

. . . I will now let my claims for decent life stand as I have made them. . . . First, a healthy body; second, an active mind in sympathy with the past, present, and the future; thirdly, occupation fit for a healthy body and an active mind; and fourthly, a beautiful world to live in . . .

. . . The mere fact that a body of men, however small, are banded together as Socialist missionaries shows that the change is going on. As the working-classes, the real organic part of society, take in these ideas, hope will arise in them, and they will claim changes in society, many of which doubtless will not tend directly towards their emancipation, because they will be claimed without due knowledge of the one thing necessary to claim, *equality of condition*; but which indirectly will help to break up our rotten sham society, while that claim for equality of condition will be made constantly and with growing loudness till it *must* be listened to, and then at last it will only be a step over the border, and the civilized world will be socialized; and, looking back at what has been, we shall be astonished to think of how long we submitted to live as we live now.

From The Commonweal   . . . If war [between Germany and France] becomes imminent our duties as Socialists are clear enough, and do not differ from those we have to act on ordinarily. To further the spread of international feeling between workers by all means possible: to point out to our own workmen that foreign competition and rivalry, or commercial war, culminating at last in open war, are necessities of the plundering classes, and that the race and commercial quarrels of these classes only concern us so far as we can use them as opportunities for fostering discontent and revolution; that the interests of the workman are the same in all countries and they can never really be enemies of each other; that the men of our labouring classes, therefore, should turn a deaf ear to the recruiting sergeant, and refuse to allow themselves to be dressed up in red and be taught to form part of the modern killing machine for the honour and glory of a country in which they have only a dog's share of many kicks and few halfpence, – all this we have to preach always, though in the event of imminent war we may have to preach it more emphatically . . .

From News from Nowhere   . . . we fell to on our breakfast, which was simple enough, but most delicately cooked, and set on the table with much daintiness. The bread was

DEMOCRATIC FEDERATION
LEAFLET

Agitate.   Educate.   Organize.

THE
DEMOCRATIC FEDERATION,
HAMMERSMITH BRANCH.

Temporary Premises:—Kelmscott House, Upper Mall, Hammersmith.

Fellow Workers,

    You are invited to join this branch, and help in spreading the principles of Socialism: some of you may be frightened at this word, and naturally so; since you have been misled and told that it means disorder and violence.

    But what is the real truth? This, that as society is now arranged there is necessarily a constant war between *Capital*, or the rich men who make profits out of work without working themselves, and *Labour*, or the poor men, who produce every thing, and have no more share in what they produce than is necessary to keep them alive and at work while they live.

    Into these two classes, rich and poor, all society is divided, and whatever profits the rich make they make at the expense of the poor, or those who are called the working classes: so also any bettering of life which the poor, or working classes, can gain, they gain at the expense of the rich.

    This is *war*, and bears with it all the waste and ruin of *war;* so that while the rich enslave the poor, they themselves are not happy, and are always trying to ruin each other.

    SOCIALISM will end this war by abolishing all classes, and making every one work for the common good; so that while every man will have the full fruits of his own labour, of which he is now deprived, he will benefit every one else by his work: this change will get rid of bad-housing, under feeding, over-work, and ignorance, and give every one a fair chance of health and happiness.

    PEACE, WELL-BEING AND ORDER, FOR ALL THEREFORE ARE THE REAL AIMS OF SOCIALISM.

    To obtain these the one thing necessary is the COMBINATION of the workers: they, who create all wealth, must learn to understand that socialism means the change from fighting each with each for life like beasts, to working together for life like men: they must get to know each other, and agree together that this change MUST be made, and then it *will* be made.

    Working-men of Hammersmith, come to the Branch and learn about those matters which to you are all important: join the Branch of the Democratic Federation, so that you may combine for real freedom, for a life fit for human beings.

    Members of the Branch meet every Monday at 8.15 p.m. for business at Kelmscott House, Upper Mall, (notice the board on the gate). Visitors are invited. All information can be obtained there as to meetings, lectures and literature of the Democratic Federation. Lectures of the Hammersmith Branch will be duly announced in " Justice," the organ of the Social Democracy.

    All communications to be addressed to the Secretary, Hammersmith Branch of the Democratic Federation, 3, Hammersmith Terrace, W.

Read "JUSTICE," *the organ of the Social Democracy*, ONE PENNY WEEKLY, *to be had of all newsmen.*

Churchman, Printer, Hammersmith.

particularly good, and was of several kinds, from the big, rather close, dark-coloured, sweet-tasting farmhouse loaf, which was most to my liking, to the thin pipe-stems of wheaten crust, such as I have eaten in Turin.

As I was putting the first mouthfuls into my mouth, my eye caught a carved and gilded inscription on the panelling, behind what we should have called the High Table in an Oxford college hall, and a familiar name in it forced me to read it through. Thus it ran:

> *'Guests and neighbours, on the site of this*
> *Guest-hall once stood the lecture-room of the*
> *Hammersmith Socialists. Drink a glass to the*
> *memory! May 1962'*

*

'Tell me one thing, if you can,' said I. 'Did the change, the "revolution" it used to be called, come peacefully?'

'Peacefully?' said he; 'what peace was there amongst those poor confused wretches of the nineteenth century? It was war from beginning to end: bitter war, till hope and pleasure put an end to it.'

'Do you mean actual fighting with weapons?' said I, 'or the strikes and lock-outs and starvation of which we have heard?'

'Both, both,' he said. 'As a matter of fact, the history of the terrible period of transition from commercial slavery to freedom may thus be summarised. When the hope of realising a communal condition of life for all men arose, quite late in the nineteenth century, the power of the middle classes, the then tyrants of society, was so enormous and crushing, that to almost all men, even those who had, you may say despite themselves, despite their reason and judgement, conceived such hopes, it seemed a dream. So much was this the case that some of those more enlightened men who were then called Socialists, although they well knew, and even stated in public, that the only reasonable condition of Society was that of pure Communism (such as you now see around you), yet shrunk from what seemed to them the barren task of preaching the realisation of a happy dream. Looking back now, we can see that the great motive-power of the change was a longing for freedom and equality . . .

'. . . the spread of communistic theories, and the partial practice of State Socialism had at first disturbed, and at last almost paralysed the marvellous system of commerce under which the old world had lived so feverishly, and had produced for some few a life of gambler's pleasure, and for many, or for most, a life of mere misery: over and over again came "bad times" as they were called, and indeed they were bad enough for the wage-slaves. The year 1952 was one of the worst of these times; the workmen suffered dreadfully: the partial, inefficient government factories, which were terribly jobbed, all but broke down, and a vast part of the population had to be fed on undisguised "charity" as it was called.'

*

I lay in my bed in my house at dingy Hammersmith thinking about it all; and trying to consider if I was overwhelmed with despair at finding I had been dreaming a dream; and strange to say, I found that I was not so despairing.

'. . . Go on living while you may, striving with whatsoever pain and labour needs must be, to build up little by little the new day of fellowship, and rest, and happiness.'

. . . if others can see it as I have seen it, then it may be called a vision rather than a dream.

From A Dream of John Ball . . . I pondered how men fight and lose the battle, and the thing that they fought for comes about in spite of their defeat, and when it comes turns out not to be what they meant, and other men have to fight for what they meant under another name . . .

The Kelmscott Press

Morris founded the Kelmscott Press, his last venture in design and craftsmanship, in 1890, the year that marked his break with the Socialist League. The Press was set up at Kelmscott House, Hammersmith, and before Morris's death in 1896 more than fifty books had been printed there, including Ruskin's On the Nature of Gothic, The Earthly Paradise *and the magnificent* Chaucer *which took four years to complete – the first two copies were delivered to Burne-Jones and Morris on 2 June 1896. William Morris died four months later.*

From A Note by William Morris on his Aims in Founding the Kelmscott Press

I began printing books with the hope of producing some which would have a definite claim to beauty, while at the same time they should be easy to read and should not dazzle the eye, or trouble the intellect of the reader by eccentricity of form in the letters. I have always been a great admirer of the calligraphy of the Middle Ages, and of the earlier printing which took its place. As to the fifteenth century books, I had noticed that they were always beautiful by force of the mere typography, even without the added ornament, with which many of them are so lavishly supplied. And it was the essence of my undertaking to produce books which it would be a pleasure to look upon as pieces of printing and arrangement of type . . .

21 NOV. 1889

To F. S. Ellis

. . . I really am thinking of turning printer myself in a small way; the first step to that would be getting new fount cut. [Emery] Walker and I both think Jenson's the best model . . . Did you ever have his Pliny? I have a vivid recollection of the vellum copy in the Bodleian.

14 SEPT. 1890

. . . As to paper I have heard of two people who may help us, one whom Walker knows and whose mill I propose to visit with Walker almost at once . . . Don't rest too much on my date of Christmas for the type: we seem to be getting on very slowly with it at present, and I have only eleven letters cut yet . . .

11 FEB. 1891

This is the state of things. The punches all cut, and matrices all struck: I had a little lot of type cast to see if any alterations were required . . . I had the g recut because it seemed to me too black. I then ordered five cwt of the type, which I am told is enough, and am expecting to have it before the end of this week or beginning of next. As soon as I get it I will set up a trial page of the Golden Legend.

BEAUVAIS, 13 AUG. 1891

To Emery Walker

. . . I have written to Prince: he has now done e i h l n o p r t. The t does not look well: I think I shall have to redesign it. The e also looks a little wrong, but might be altered. The rest looks very well indeed . . .

THE FINAL YEARS

From Mackail
'Tuesday I went to bury my mother . . . a pleasant winter day with gleams of sun. She was laid in earth in the churchyard close by the house, a very pretty place among the great wych elms, which, if it were of no use to her, was softening to us. Altogether my old and callous heart was touched by the absence of what had been so kind to me and fond of me. She was eighty-nine, and had been ill for nearly four years.'

KELMSCOTT MANOR, AUG. 1895

To Georgiana
. . . It was a most lovely afternoon when I came down here, and I was prepared to enjoy the journey from Oxford to Lechlade very much: and so I did; but woe's me! when we passed by the once lovely little garth near Black Bourton, I saw all my worst fears realized; for there was the little barn we saw being mended, the wall cut down and finished with a zinked iron roof. It quite sickened me when I saw it. That's the way all things are going now. In twenty years everything will be gone in this countryside, which twenty years ago was so rich in beautiful building: and we can do nothing to help it or mend it . . . In the meantime I can do nothing but a little bit of Anti-Scrape – *sweet to the eye while seen*. Now that I am grown old and see that nothing is to be done, I half wish I had not been born with a sense of romance and beauty in this accursed age. . . .

4 OCT. 1895

To the Editor, The Daily Chronicle
. . . In these days when history is studied so keenly through genuine original documents, and has thereby gained a vitality which makes it such a contrast to the dull and not too veracious accounts of kings and nobles, that used to do duty for history, it seems pitiable indeed that the most important documents of all, the ancient buildings of Middle Ages, the work of associated labour and thought of the *people*, the result of a chain of tradition unbroken from the earliest stages of art, should be falsified by an uneasy desire to do something, a vulgar craving for formal completeness, which is almost essentially impossible in a building that has grown from decade to decade and century to century . . .

KELMSCOTT MANOR, 27 APRIL 1896

To Philip Webb
I said I would write to you and tell you how I was getting on so here goes. . . . I don't seem to mend a bit, am weak and belly-achy. Let that pass. Otherwise all is well. I have been enjoying the garden much: as one walks about and about there is no eyesore: all is beautiful. You are right about the grass; it is well grown and as green as green. Also the apple-blossom . . . is very fine, I don't think we at K. ever had so

much. We are rather between the flowers, but the tulips are coming on thick, and the wall-flowers are splendid . . . The rooks are very musical, but I have heard the blackbirds stronger. I only hear the cuckoo about 7 a.m. . . .

18 AUG. 1896

My dear Fellow. I am back [from a visit to Norway]. Please come and see me. I saw Throndhjem – big church, terribly restored, but well worth seeing; in fact, as beautiful as can be. It quite touched my hard heart.

PS Somewhat better, but hated the voyage; so glad to be home.

KELMSCOTT HOUSE, 20 AUG. 1896

To Jenny   I am so distressed I cannot get down to Kelmscott on Saturday; but I am not well, & the doctors will not let me; please my own dear forgive me, for I long to see you with all my heart. I hope to get down early next week darling. I send you my very best love . . .

KELMSCOTT HOUSE, 26 AUG. 1896

To Thomas Wardle   It is very kind of you to invite me to share in your paradise, and I am absolutely delighted to find another beautiful place which is still in its untouched loveliness. I should have certainly accepted your invitation, but am quite unable to do so, for at present I cannot walk over the threshold, being so intensely weak. The Manifold is the same river, is it not, which you carried me across on your back, which situation tickled us so much that, owing to inextinguishable laughter, you very nearly dropped me in. What pleasant old times those were.

1 SEPT. 1896

To Georgiana   . . . Come soon, I want a sight of your dear face.

From A Dream of John Ball   '. . . though I die and end, yet mankind liveth, therefore I end not, since I am a man . . .'

From Mackail   On the morning of Saturday the 3rd of October, between eleven and twelve o'clock, he died quietly and without visible suffering.

William Morris was buried in the churchyard at Kelmscott on 6 October. His coffin was carried on a hay cart through the country lanes to the church, which was decorated for the Harvest Festival. Philip Webb, who had built his first home, made him his last one – a coped tomb-stone in the local Cotswold tradition.

DESIGN FOR A CEILING, *c.* 1880

HAMMERSMITH RUG, *c.* 1880

HAMMERSMITH RUNNER, *c.* 1880

THE FOREST TAPESTRY, 1887

now sit and see · nor ride nor haste

DESIGN FOR ST. JAMES'S, 1881

ST. JAMES'S WALLPAPER, 1881

DESIGN FOR ROSE AND THISTLE, 1882

ROSE AND THISTLE PRINTED COTTON, 1882

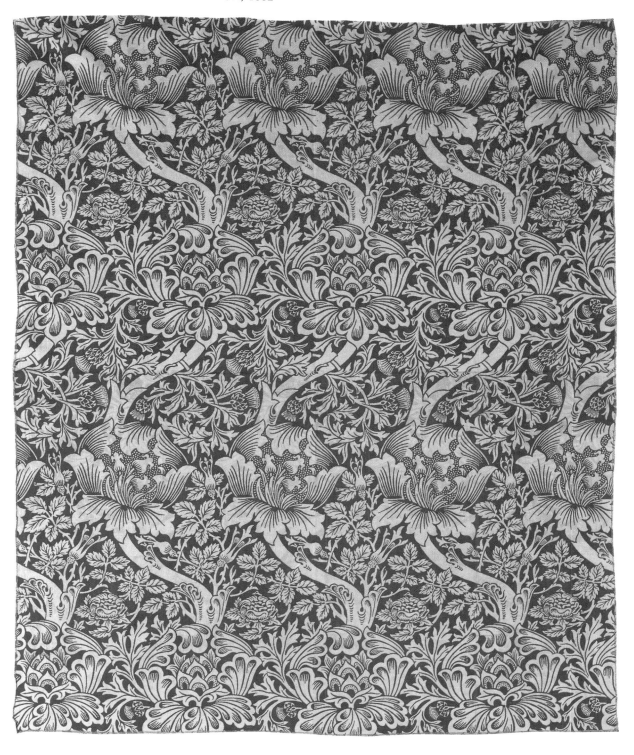

WOODBLOCK FOR BIRD AND ANEMONE, *c.* 1881

BIRD AND ANEMONE PRINTED COTTON, 1882

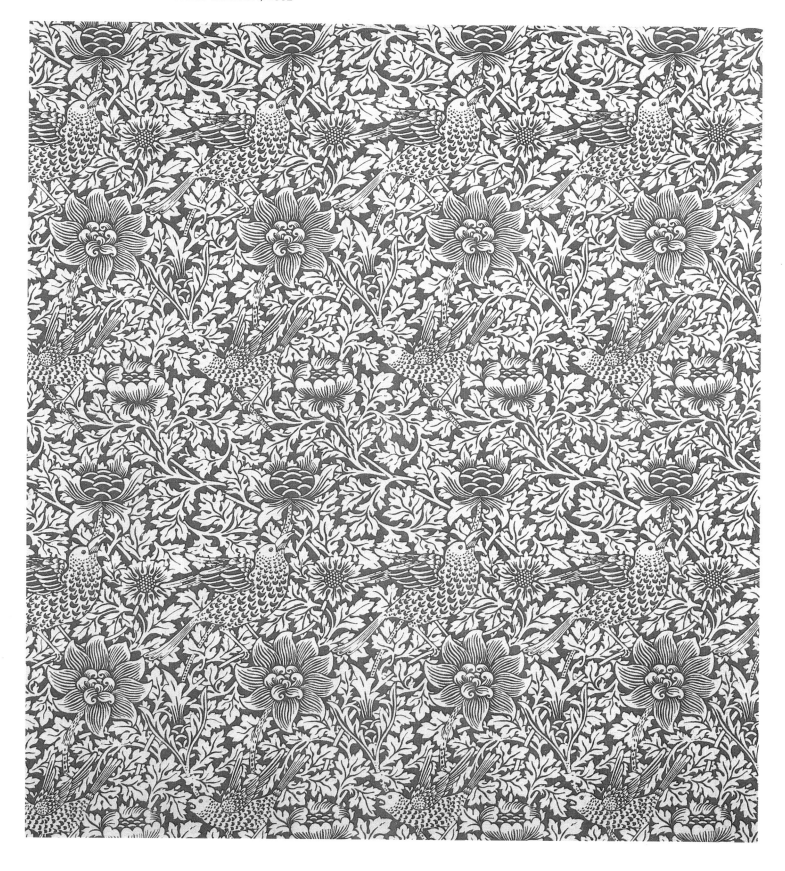

DESIGN FOR A RUG,
DATE UNKNOWN

DESIGN FOR REDCAR CARPET, *c.* 1881—5

VIOLET AND COLUMBINE WOVEN FABRIC, 1883

BRER RABBIT OR BROTHER RABBIT PRINTED COTTON, 1882

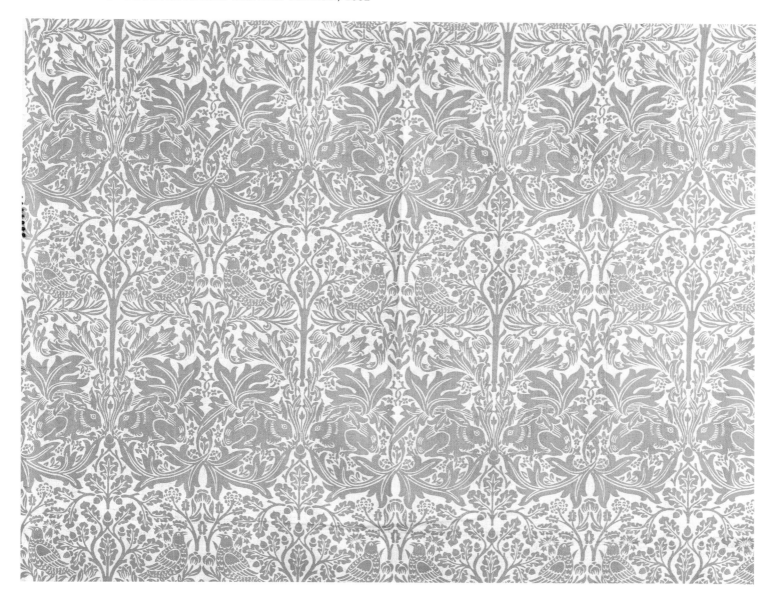

c. 1880–1896

SOUTH AISLE WINDOW, ST. PETER AND ST. PAUL,
CATTISTOCK, DORSET, 1882

MINSTREL ANGEL WITH ORGAN, 1882

A MINSTREL ANGEL WITH T-SHAPED DULCIMER, 1882

A CENSING ANGEL, 1882

BULLERSWOOD CARPET, *c.* 1889

HOLLAND PARK CARPET, *c.* 1887

DESIGN FOR PATCHWORK EMBROIDERY, DATE UNKNOWN

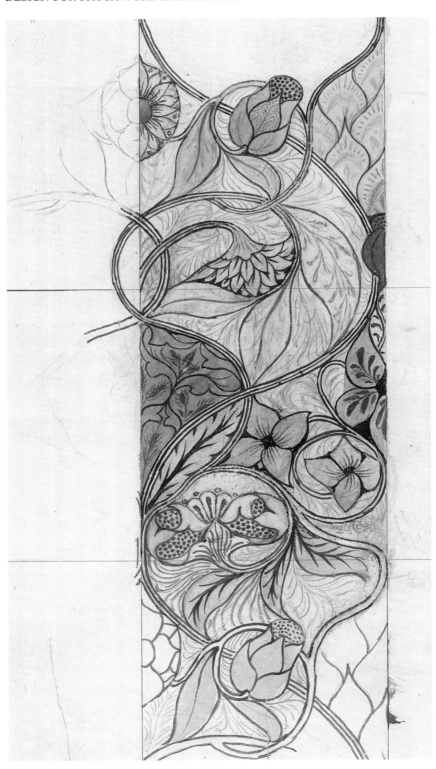

CORNCOCKLE PRINTED COTTON, 1883

DESIGN FOR PRINTED FABRIC, DATE UNKNOWN

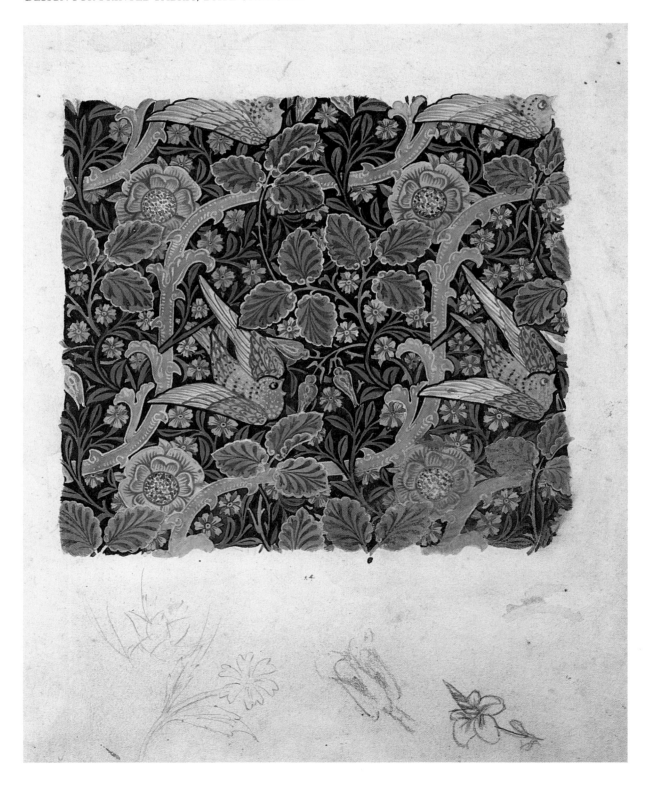

STRAWBERRY THIEF PRINTED COTTON, 1883

DESIGN FOR WEY, *c.* 1883

WEY PRINTED COTTON, *c.* 1883

DESIGN FOR EVENLODE, 1883

EVENLODE PRINTED COTTON, 1883

WORKING DRAWING FOR KENNET, 1883

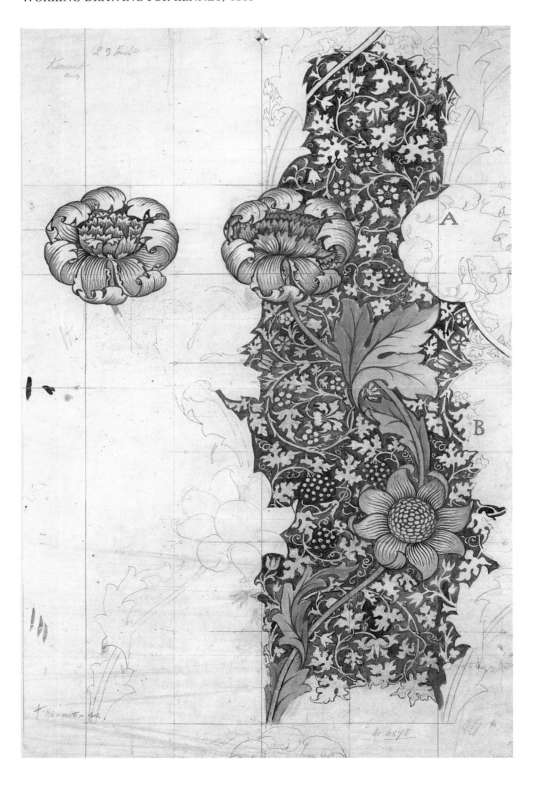

KENNET PRINTED COTTON, 1883

WOODBLOCK FOR KENNET, 1883

KENNET SILK DAMASK, 1883

DESIGN FOR WINDRUSH, 1883

WINDRUSH PRINTED COTTON, 1883

DESIGN FOR GRAFTON, 1883

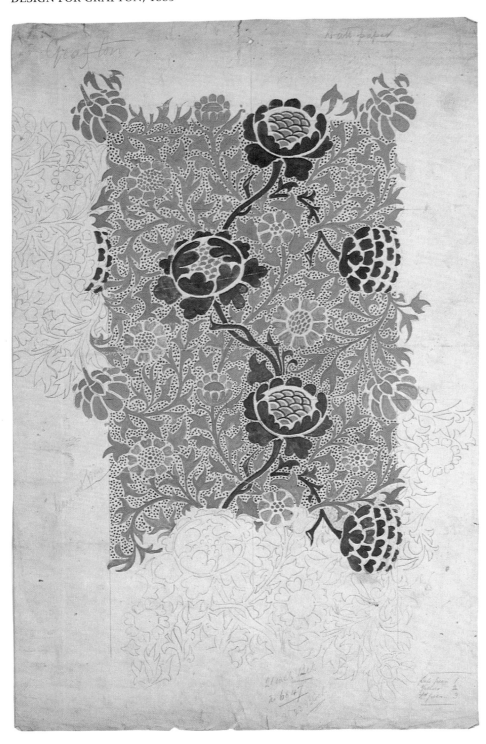

GRAFTON WALLPAPER, 1883

DESIGN FOR FLOWERPOTS, 1883

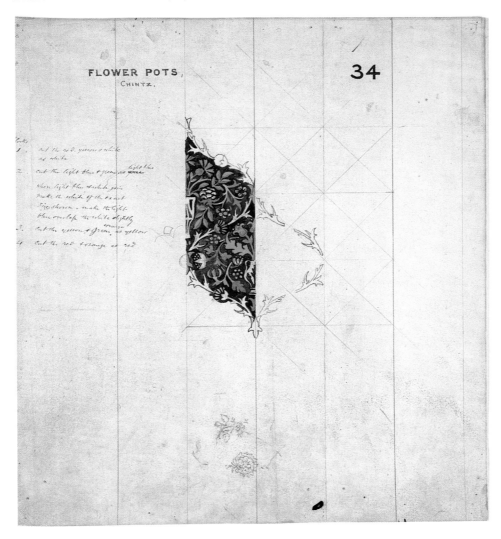

FLOWERPOTS PRINTED COTTON, 1883

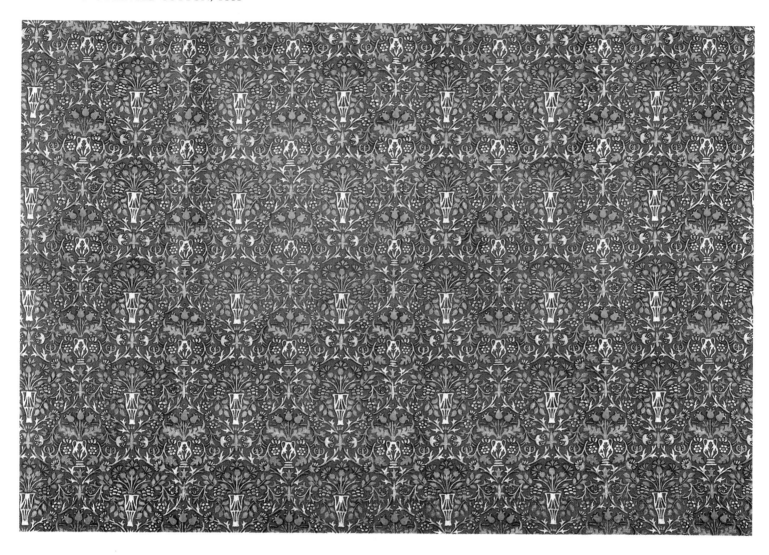

DESIGN FOR EYEBRIGHT, 1883

EYEBRIGHT PRINTED COTTON, 1883

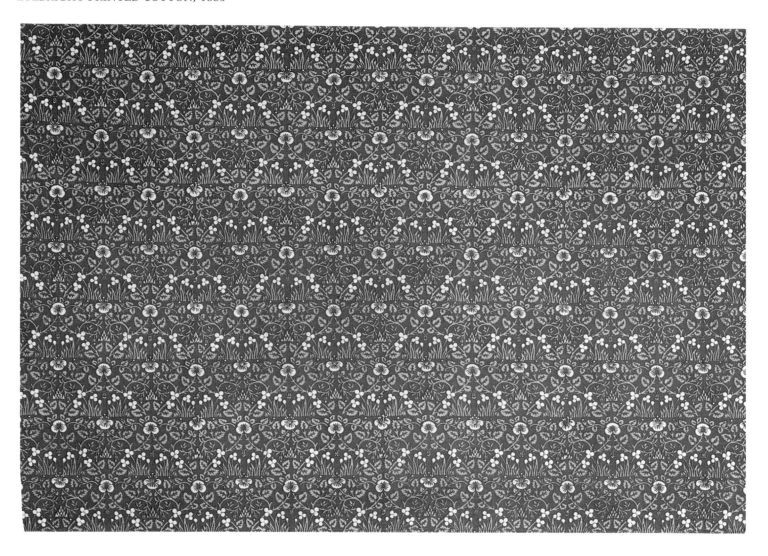

c. 1880–1896

CRAY PRINTED COTTON, 1884

WANDLE PRINTED COTTON, 1884

270

DESIGN FOR COTTON DAMASK, DATE UNKNOWN

GRANADA WOVEN SILK AND VELVET, 1884

LODDEN PRINTED COTTON, 1884

DINING ROOM, WIGHTWICK MANOR, STAFFORDSHIRE

DESIGN FOR A TAPESTRY, DATE UNKNOWN

WOODPECKER TAPESTRY, 1885

DRAWING FOR MEDWAY, 1885

MEDWAY PRINTED COTTON, 1885

LILY AND POMEGRANATE WALLPAPER, 1886

DESIGN FOR LILY AND POMEGRANATE, 1886

BALMORAL WALLPAPER, 1887

LEA PRINTED COTTON, 1885

ORCHARD TAPESTRY, 1890

GREENERY

DESIGN FOR ORCHARD
TAPESTRY, 1890

valiant earth o happy year and hangs aloft from tree to tree
that works the threat of winter year the banners of the spring to be

DESIGN FOR PAINTED DECORATION, STANMORE HALL, MIDDLESEX, 1888

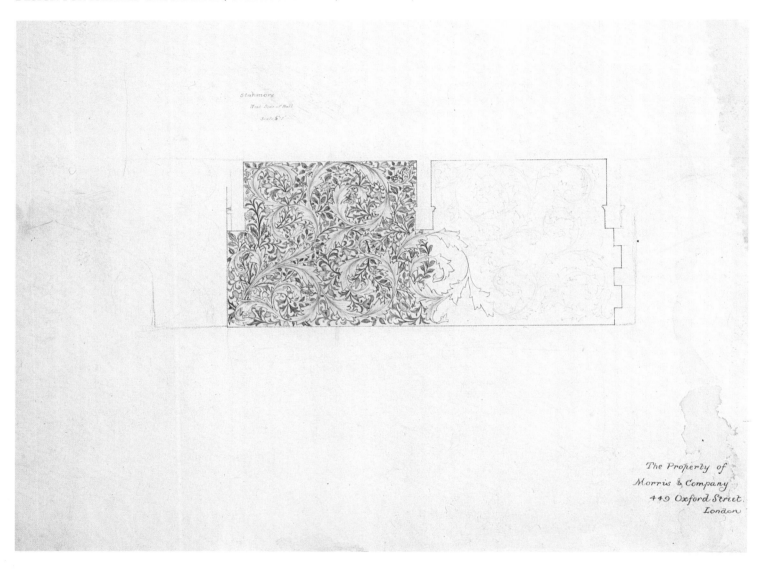

WILLOW BOUGHS WALLPAPER, 1887

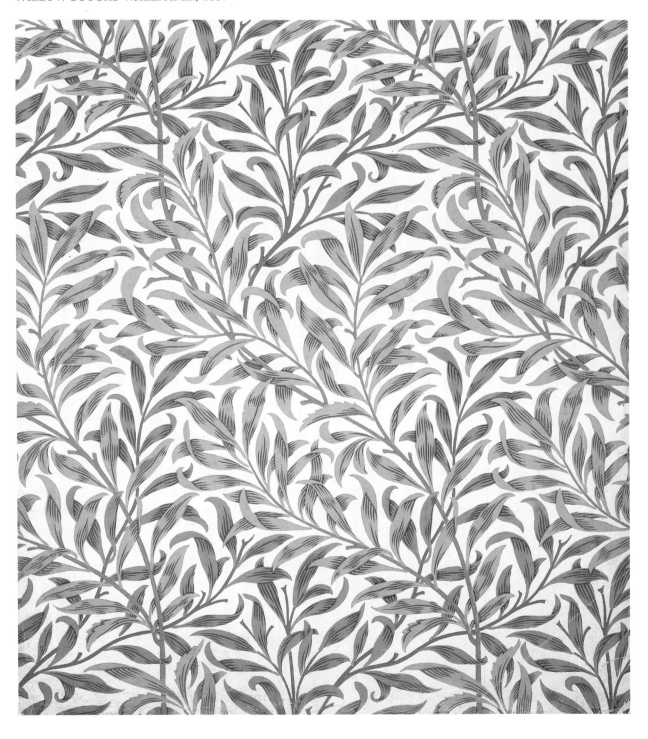

GOLDEN BOUGH WOVEN SILK, 1888

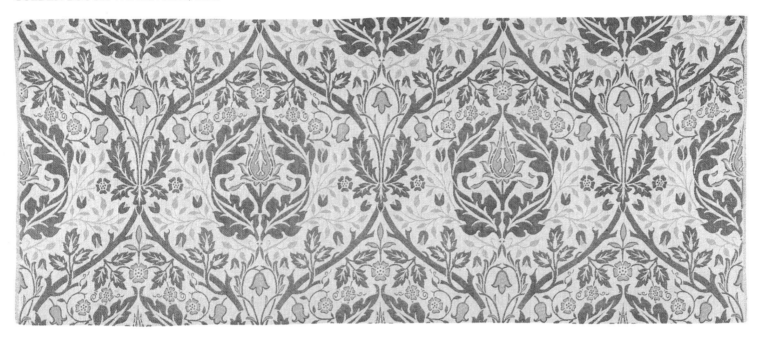

ISPHAHAN WOVEN WOOL, *c.* 1888

WOODBLOCK FOR PINK AND ROSE WALLPAPER, *c.* 1890

PINK AND ROSE WALLPAPER, 1891

THE PINK & ROSE. MORRIS & C.º

VERDURE (FOR HOLY GRAIL TAPESTRY), *c.* 1900

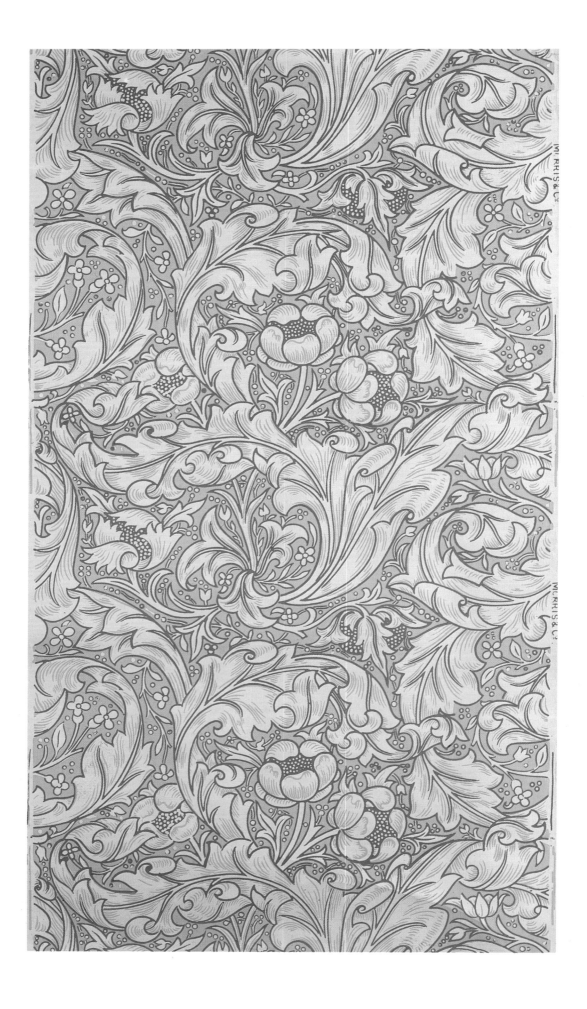

BACHELOR'S BUTTON WALLPAPER, *c.* 1892

SHOWCASE AND LANDING, STANDEN

NEWS FROM NOWHERE, TITLE PAGE PROOF, *c.* 1892

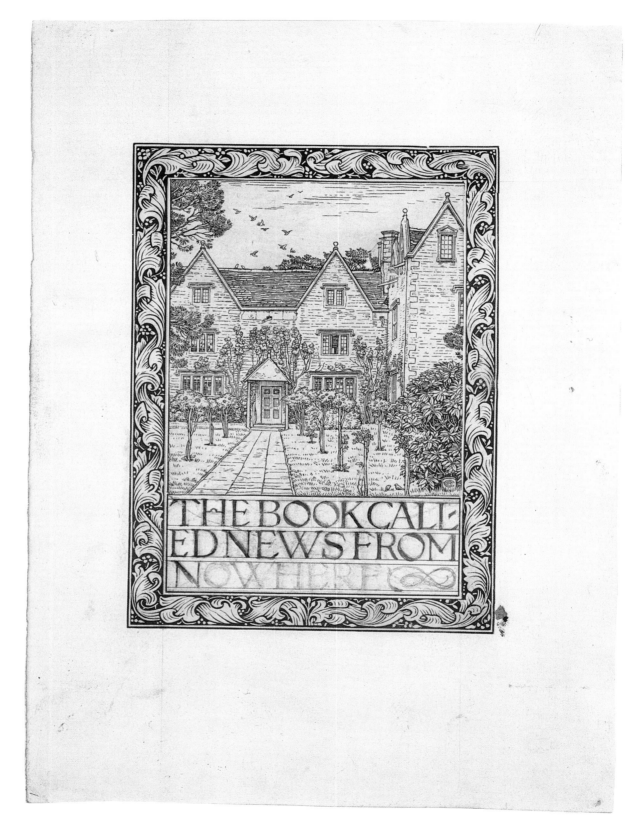

NEWS FROM NOWHERE, FRONTISPIECE, 1892

THIS IS THE PICTURE OF THE OLD HOUSE BY THE THAMES TO WHICH THE PEOPLE OF THIS STORY WENT. HEREAFTER FOLLOWS THE BOOK IT. SELF WHICH IS CALLED NEWS FROM NOWHERE OR AN EPOCH OF REST & IS WRITTEN BY WILLIAM MORRIS.

NEWS FROM NOWHERE OR AN EPOCH OF REST. CHAPTER I. DISCUSSION AND BED.

UP at the League, says a friend, there had been one night a brisk conversational discussion, as to what would happen on the Morrow of the Revolution, finally shading off into a vigorous statement by various friends, of their views on the future of the fully-developed new society.

SAYS our friend: Considering the subject, the discussion was good-tempered; for those present, being used to public meetings & after-lecture debates, if they did not listen to each other's opinions, which could scarcely be expected of them, at all events did not always attempt to speak all together, as is the custom of people in ordinary polite society when conversing

A DREAM OF JOHN BALL, FRONTISPIECE, 1892

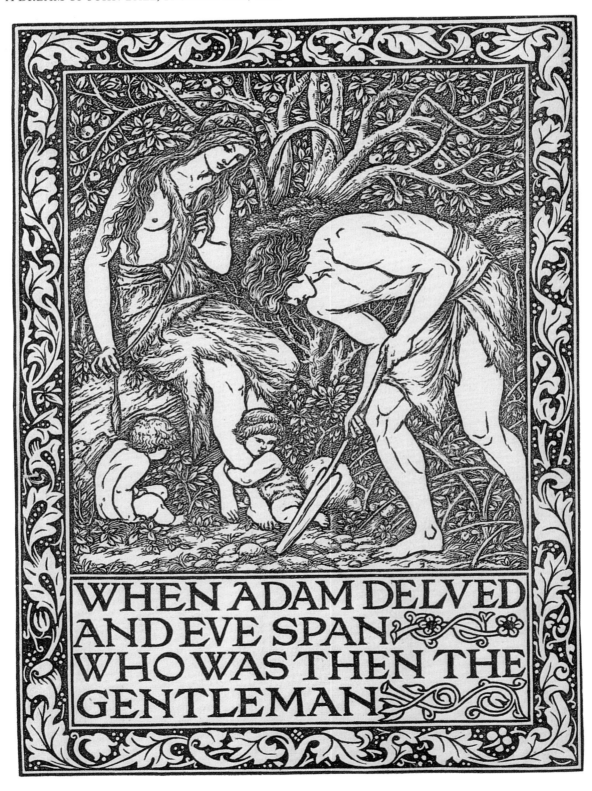

WHEN ADAM DELVED
AND EVE SPAN
WHO WAS THEN THE
GENTLEMAN

FIRST PAGE PRINTED AT THE KELMSCOTT PRESS, 1891

HF old man answered not a word, and he seemed to be a-sleep, and Hallblithe deemed that his cheeks were ruddier and his skin less wasted and wrin-kled than aforetime. Then spake one of these women : Fear not, young man ; he is well and will soon be better. Her voice was as sweet as a spring bird in the morn-ing ; she was white-skinned and dark-haired, and full sweetly fashioned ; and she laughed on Hallblithe, but not mockingly; and her fel-lows also laughed as though it were strange for him to be there. Then they did on there shoon again, and with the carle laid their hands to the bed whereon the old man lay, and lifted him up, and bore him forth on to the grass, turning their faces towards the flowery wood aforesaid ; and they went a little way and then laid him down again and rested; and so on little by little, till they had brought him to the edge of the wood, and still he seemed to be a-sleep. Then the damsel who had spoken be-fore, she with the dark hair, said to allblithe: " Although we have gazed on thee as if in wonder, this it not because we did not look to meet thee, but because thou art so fair and goodly a man : so abide thou here till we come back to thee from out of the wood."
Therewith she stroked his hand, and with her

First page printed at the Kelmscott Press Jan 31 1891
see p.12
note use of g immediately discarded.

THE GOLDEN LEGEND, DESIGN FOR TITLE PAGE, 1892

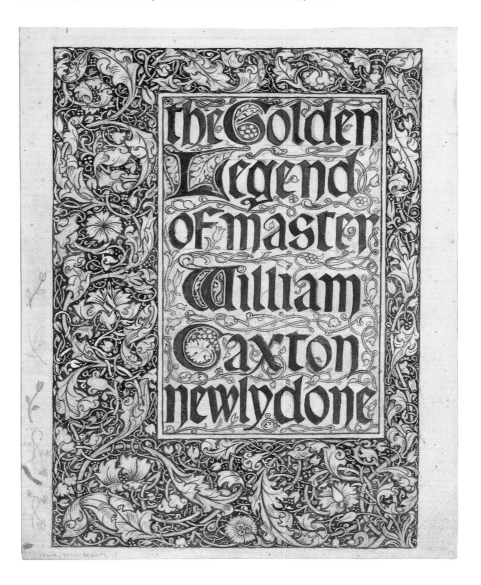

PAGES FROM *THE GOLDEN LEGEND,* 1892

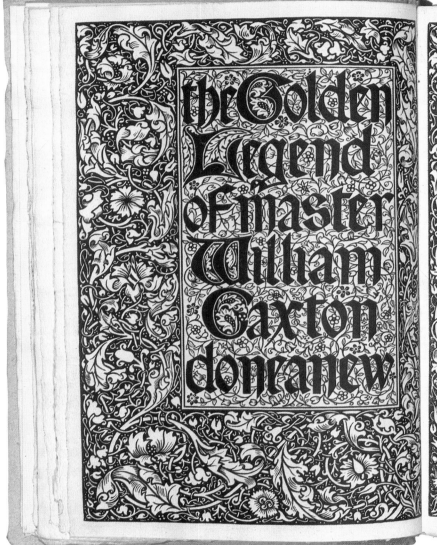

PAGE FROM THE RUBEUS *HISTORICA FIORENTINA* COPIED BY WILLIAM MORRIS, *c*. 1892

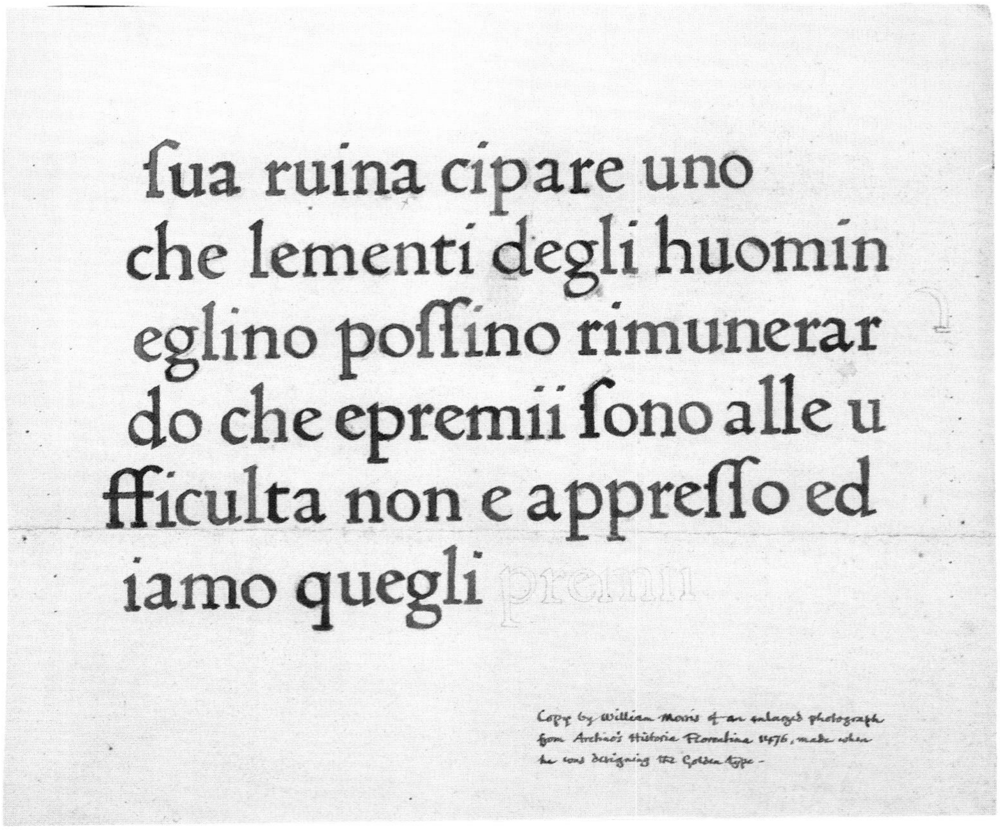

ſua ruina cipare uno
che lementi degli huomin
eglino poſſino rimunerar
do che epremii ſono alle u
fficulta non e appreſſo ed
iamo quegli premii

Copy by William Morris of an enlarged photograph
from Rubeus's Historia Florentina 1476, made when
he was designing the Golden type.

THE RECUYELL OF THE HYSTORYES OF TROYE, TITLE PAGE, 1892

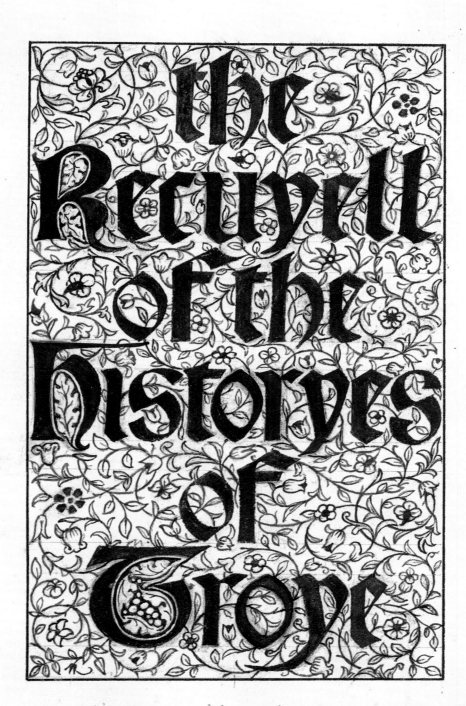

Original design by William Morris for the titlepage.

PAGE FROM *SONNETS AND LYRICAL POEMS* BY DANTE GABRIEL ROSSETTI, 1894

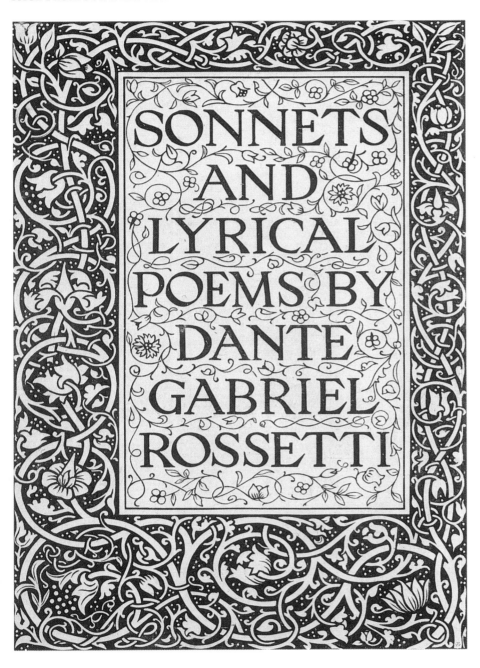

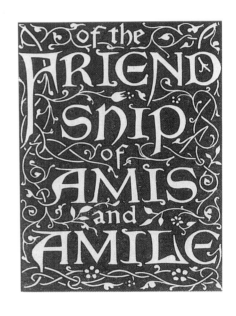

PAGE FROM *THE TALE OF BEOWULF,* 1895

VII. Beowulf speaketh with Hrothgar, and telleth how
he will meet Grendel.

ORD then gave out Hrothgar, the helm of
the Scyldings.
I knew him in sooth when he was but a
youngling,
And his father, the old man, was
Ecgtheow hight;
Unto whom at his home gave Hrethel the Geat/lord
His one only daughter; and now hath his offspring
All hardy come hither a lief lord to seek him.
For that word they spake then, the sea/faring men,
E'en they who the gift/scat for the Geat/folk had ferry'd,
Brought thither for thanks, that of thirty of men/folk
The craft of might hath he within his own hand/grip,
That war/strong of men. Now him holy God
for kind help hath sent off here even to us,
We men of the West Danes, as now I have weening,
'Gainst the terror of Grendel. So I to that good one
for his mighty mood/daring shall the dear treasure bid.
Haste now and be speedy, and bid them in straightway,
The kindred/band gather'd together, to see us,
And in words say thou eke that they be well comen
To the folk of the Danes. To the door of the hall then
Went Wulfgar, and words withinward he flitted:
E bade me to say you, my lord of fair battle,
The Ealdor of East/Danes, that he your blood
knoweth
And that unto him are ye, the sea/surges over,
Ye lads hardy/hearted, well come to land hither;
And now may ye wend you all in war/raiment

DESIGN FOR TROY TYPE, 1891

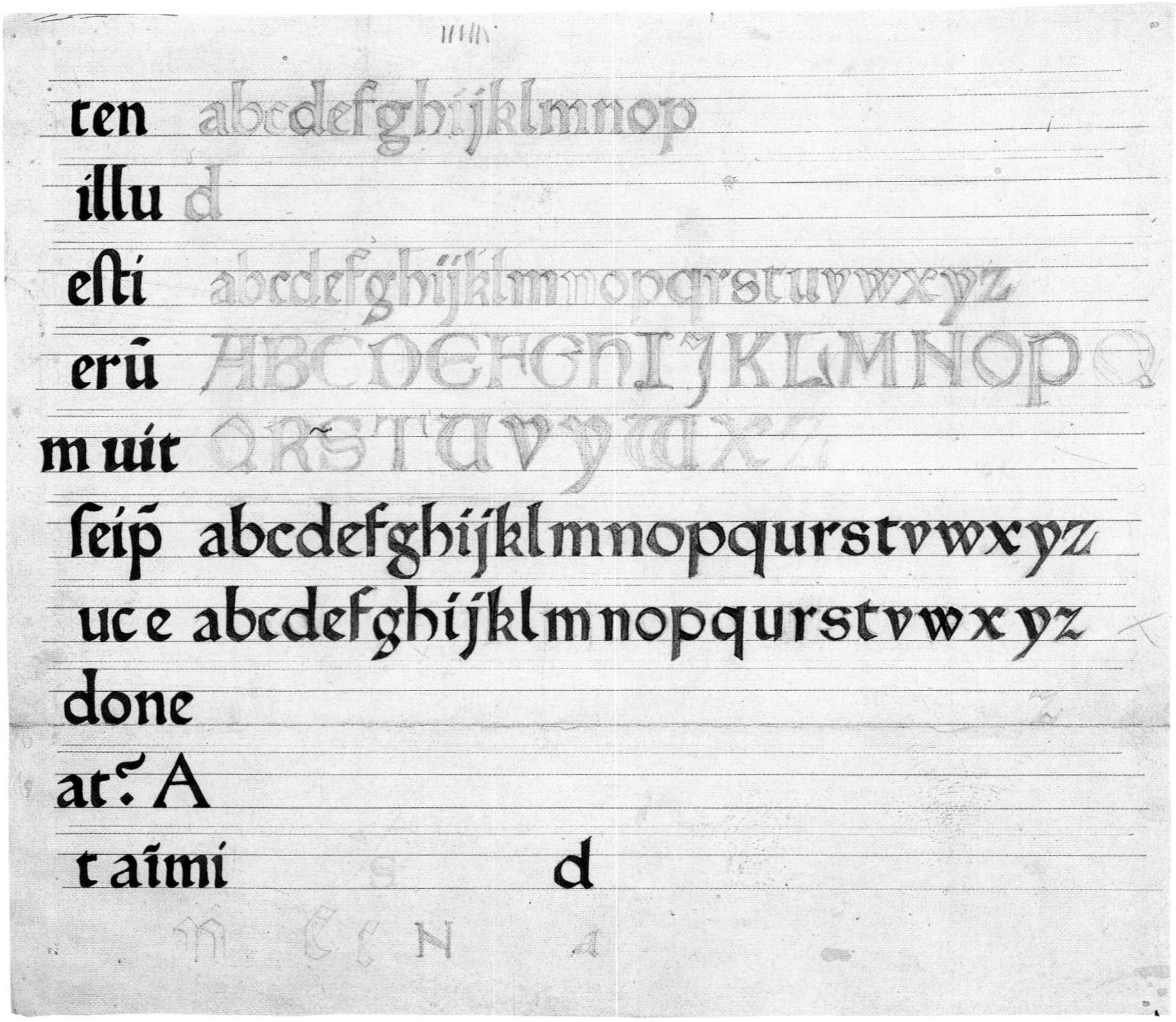

DESIGN FOR BORDER ORNAMENT, *THE EARTHLY PARADISE*, 1866

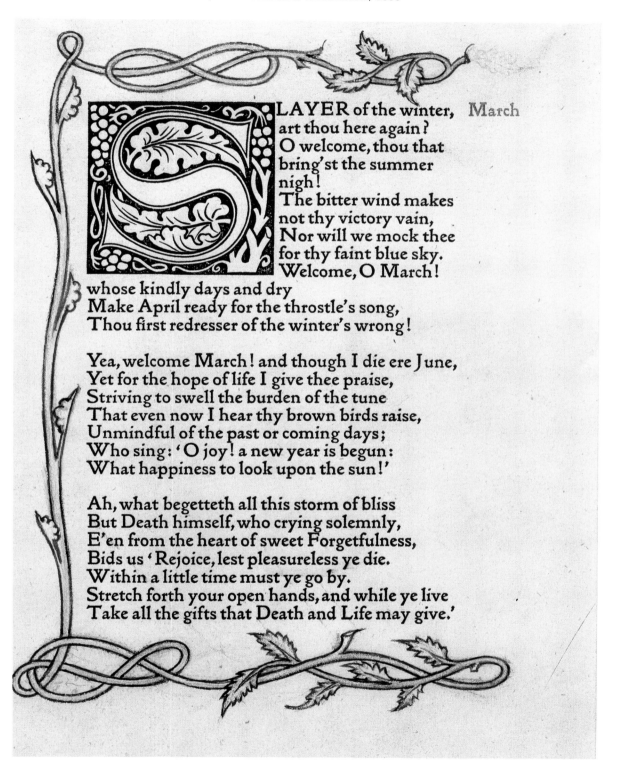

LAYER of the winter, March
art thou here again?
O welcome, thou that
bring'st the summer
nigh!
The bitter wind makes
not thy victory vain,
Nor will we mock thee
for thy faint blue sky.
Welcome, O March!
whose kindly days and dry
Make April ready for the throstle's song,
Thou first redresser of the winter's wrong!

Yea, welcome March! and though I die ere June,
Yet for the hope of life I give thee praise,
Striving to swell the burden of the tune
That even now I hear thy brown birds raise,
Unmindful of the past or coming days;
Who sing: 'O joy! a new year is begun:
What happiness to look upon the sun!'

Ah, what begetteth all this storm of bliss
But Death himself, who crying solemnly,
E'en from the heart of sweet Forgetfulness,
Bids us 'Rejoice, lest pleasureless ye die.
Within a little time must ye go by.
Stretch forth your open hands, and while ye live
Take all the gifts that Death and Life may give.'

DESIGN FOR SPECIAL BINDING, THE KELMSCOTT *CHAUCER*, 1895

SPECIAL BINDING FOR THE KELMSCOTT *CHAUCER*, 1896

PAGES FROM THE KELMSCOTT *CHAUCER*, 1896

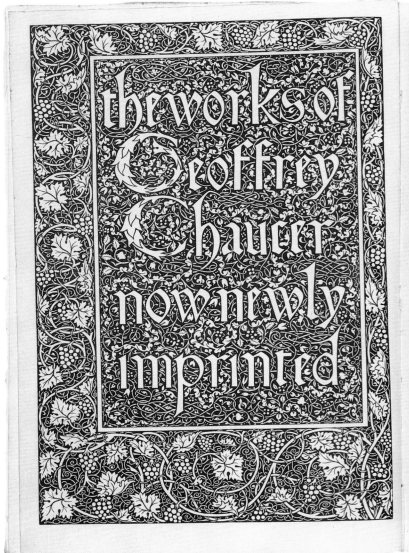

PAGES FROM THE KELMSCOTT *CHAUCER*, 1896

WILLIAM MORRIS BY OTHERS

Robert Blatchford in Clarion, *October 1896*   I cannot help thinking that it does not matter what goes into the *Clarion* this week, because William Morris is dead. And what Socialist will care for any other news this week, beyond that one sad fact? He was our best man, and he is dead . . .

It is true that much of his work still lives, and will live. But we have lost him, and, great as was his work, he himself was greater . . . he was better than his best. Though his words fell like sword strokes, one always felt that the warrior was stronger than his sword. For Morris was not only a genius, he was a *man*. Strike at him where you would, he rang true . . .

. . . He was our best man. We cannot spare him; we cannot replace him. In all England there lives no braver, kinder, honester, cleverer, heartier man than William Morris. He is dead, and we cannot help feeling for a while that nothing else matters . . .

Edward Carpenter in Freedom, *December 1896*   . . . One of the last times I heard him speak in public was in 1889, at the Paris Socialist Congress. After the glib oratorical periods . . . what a contrast to see Morris – in navy-blue pilot suit – fighting furiously there on the platform with his own words (he was not feeling well that day), hacking and hewing the stubborn English phrases out – his tangled grey mane tossing, his features reddening with the effort! But the effect was remarkable. Something in the solid English way of looking at things, the common-sense and practical outlook on the world, the earnestness and tenacity, as of a skipper beating up against the wind and the wave on the great deep, made that speech one of the most effective in the session . . .

Walter Crane in Progressive Review, *November 1896* . . . that the 'idle singer of an empty day' should voice the claims and hopes of labour, stand up for the rights of free speech in Trafalgar Square, and speak from a waggon in Hyde Park, may have surprised those who only knew him upon one side; but to those who fully apprehended the reality, ardour, and sincerity of his nature, such action was but its logical outcome and complement, and assuredly it redounds to the honour of the artist, the scholar, and the poet whose loss we mourn today, that he was also a man.

W.B. Yeats in Bookman, *November 1896*   . . . In the literal sense of the word, and in the only high sense, he was a prophet; and it was his vision of that perfect life, which the world is always trying . . . to bring forth, that awakened every activity of his laborious life – his revival of medieval tapestry and stained glass, his archaic printing, his dreams of Sigurd and of Gudrun and of Guinevere, his essays on the unloveliness of our life and art, his preaching in parks and at the corners of streets, his praise of revolutions, his marchings at the head of crowds, and his fierce anger against most things that we delight to honour . . .

QUOTING R.W. DIXON (LATER CANON DIXON)

J.W. Mackail, The Life of William Morris *(1899)* . . . At first Morris was regarded by the Pembroke [College, Oxford] men simply as a very pleasant boy . . . who was fond of talking, which he did in a great husky shout, and fond of going down the river . . . In no long time, however, the great characters of his nature began to impress us. His fire and impetuosity, great bodily strength, and high temper were soon manifested; and were sometimes astonishing. As. *e.g.*, his habit of beating his own head, dealing himself vigorous blows, to take it out of himself. I think it was he who brought in singlestick, I remember him offering to 'teach the cuts and guards.' But his mental qualities, his intellect, also began to be perceived and acknowledged. I remember Faulkner remarking to me, 'How Morris seems to know things, doesn't he?' And then it struck me that it was so. I observed how decisive he was: how accurate, without any effort or formality: what an extraordinary power of observation lay at the base of many of his casual or incidental remarks, and how many things he knew that were quite out of our way; as, *e.g.*, architecture . . .

. . . One night, Crom Price and I went to Exeter [College], and found him with Burne-Jones. As soon as we entered the room, Burne-Jones exclaimed wildly, "He's a big poet." "Who is?" asked we. "Why, Topsy" – the name which he had given him. This name, given from his mass of dark, curly hair, and generally unkempt appearance, stuck to Morris among the circle of his intimate friends all his life. It was frequently shortened into "Top".

Mackail   The idea that poetry could, or should, be cultivated as an isolated and specific product, or that towards its production it was desirable to isolate one's self from common interests and occupations, and stand a little apart from all the turmoils or trivialities of common life, was one which he found not so much untrue as unintelligible. 'If a chap can't compose an epic poem while he's weaving tapestry,' he once said, 'he had better shut up, he'll never do any good at all.'

Letters of 1867 from Warington Taylor to Rossetti, in Rossetti Papers

As to Morris having his capital, keep him without it; he will only spend it in books. In about three years time it will be of use to him for publishing purposes: at the present it would go on wine and books!!! . . .

. . . Morris will start half a dozen jobs: he only has designs perhaps for half of them, and therefore in a week or two they will be given up. They are put away, bits get lost, have to be done over again: hence great loss of time and money.

Morris and I never get hot with one another save on the subject of price. He is always for a low price: seeing the amount of work we do it is absurd. We must have a long price . . . I am always fighting, and have generally managed to get my own way with a swear and curse . . . Another point in this: Morris and Ned will do no work except by driving, and you must keep up the supply of designs . . .

Mackail   In his suit of blue serge and soft felt hat [1870], he had something of the look of a working engineer and something of that of a sailor. He was walking down Kensington High Street one morning when a fireman from the brigade station stopped him and said, 'Beg pardon, sir, but were you ever captain of the Sea Swallow?'

QUOTING EDWARD BURNE-JONES

'From the first I knew how different he was from all the men I had ever met. He talked with vehemence and sometimes with violence. I never knew him languid or tired. He was slight in figure in those days [1853]; his hair was dark brown and very thick, his nose straight, his eyes hazel-coloured, his mouth exceedingly delicate and beautiful.'

. . . a photograph of about this period [1856] . . . also shows the characteristic hands – broad, fleshy, and rather short, with a look about them of clumsiness and ineffectiveness which was absolutely the reverse of the truth. It was a perpetual amazement to see those hands executing the most delicately minute work with a swiftness and precision that no one else could equal . . .

'. . . in the thick of his work, it was noticeable how he never seemed to be particularly busy, and how he had plenty of leisure for expeditions, for fishing, for amusement, if it amused him; he never seemed to read much, but always knew, and accurately; and he had a great instinct at all times for knowing what would not amuse him, and what not to read.'

Georgiana Burne-Jones, Memorials   He was very handsome, of an unusual type – the statues of medieval kings often remind me of him – and at that time [1856] he wore no moustache, so that the drawing of his mouth, which was his most expressive feature, could be clearly seen. His eyes always seemed to take in rather than to give out. His hair waved and curled triumphantly.

From The Letters of Henry James (*1920*)   . . . There was something very quaint and remote from actual life, it seemed to me, in the whole scene: Morris reading in his flowing antique numbers a legend of prodigies and terrors . . . around us all the picturesque bric-a-brac of the apartment (every article of furniture literally a 'specimen' of something or other) and in the corner this dark, silent medieval woman with her medieval toothache. Morris himself is extremely pleasant and quite different from his wife. He impressed me most agreeably. He is short, burly, corpulent, very careless and unfinished in his dress . . . He has a very loud voice and a nervous, restless manner and a perfectly unaffected and business-like address.

His talk indeed is wonderfully to the point and remarkable for clear, good sense... He's an extraordinary example, in short, of a delicate sensitive genius and taste, saved by a perfectly healthy body and temper.

Richard Norman Shaw　　　　　　　　　　　William Morris was a great man who somehow delighted in
　　　glaring wallpapers.

Peter Floud, 'The Wallpaper Designs of William Morris'. Penrose Annual, *Vol. 24, 1960*
　　　　　　　　　　　　　　　... there can be little doubt that at every stage in his development Morris's best papers demonstrate an instinctive mastery of the art of pattern designing hardly reached by even the cleverest of his contemporaries, and bear a classic imprint quite lacking in papers which in their day must have seemed much more *avant-garde*. It is just this timeless quality which makes one confident that sooner or later some enterprising manufacturer will decide to put a selection of Morris's designs back on the market again.

E.P. Thompson, William Morris, Romantic to Revolutionary *(1955)*
　　　　　　　　　　　　　William Morris was the first creative artist of major stature in the world to take his stand, consciously and without shadow of compromise, with the revolutionary working-class: to participate in the day-to-day work of building the Socialist movement: to put his brain and his genius at its disposal in the struggle.

　　It is no small matter for a man of fifty, in the face of the ridicule of society, the indifference of wife and friends, to set aside the work he loves and fashion his life anew. But this is what he did...

F.R. Leavis, New Bearings in English Poetry *(1954, 2nd edn)*
　　　　　　　　　　　　　William Morris was one of the most versatile, energetic and original men of his time, a force that impinged decisively on the world of practice.

E.P. Thompson, William Morris, Romantic to Revolutionary
　　　　　　　　　　　　　　　... So he still paces ahead of us, no longer 'lonely' but still in the van – beckoning us forward to the measureless bounty of life. He is one of those men whom history will never overtake.

GUIDE TO THE PRINCIPAL PERSONALITIES MENTIONED IN THE TEXT

WILLIAM ALLINGHAM (1824–1889). Poet and writer; friend of Rossetti, *q.v.*, and Morris. Editor *Fraser's Magazine*.

LOUISA BALDWIN (1845–1925). Née Macdonald; sister of Georgiana Burne-Jones, *q.v.* Married Alfred Baldwin; their son, Stanley, was Conservative Prime Minister in the 1920s and 1930s.

GEORGE FREDERICK BODLEY (1827–1907). Architect (St Michael and All Angels, Brighton, All Saints, Selsely, and Jesus College, Cambridge); one of the first patrons of the Firm.

FORD MADOX BROWN (1821–1893). Painter associated with the Pre-Raphaelite Brotherhood. Founder member of Morris, Marshall, Faulkner & Co.; designed some furniture and stained glass for the Firm, but ceased to work for it when Morris took over in 1875.

ELIZABETH BURDEN (BESSY) (b. 1842). Jane Morris's youngest sister; lived with the family and became a skilled embroiderer, working for the Firm, and helping to keep the accounts.

JANE BURDEN, see Jane Morris.

EDWARD BURNE-JONES (1833–1898). Painter and life-long friend of Morris; they met as undergraduates in Exeter College, Oxford. Burne-Jones was a founder member of Morris, Marshall, Faulkner & Co., and worked for the Firm throughout his career, designing most of the figures for the stained glass and tapestries. He also produced illustrations for the Kelmscott Press. Often referred to as 'Ted' or 'Ned'. Married Georgiana, née Macdonald, *q.v.* in 1860, and lived at The Grange in Hammersmith, and at Rottingdean in Sussex.

GEORGIANA BURNE-JONES (1840–1920). Friend and confidante of William Morris (who wrote and illuminated *A Book of Verse* for her in 1870). One of five remarkable sisters (including Louisa Baldwin, *q.v.*) all of whom married or were mothers of famous men; her nephews included Stanley Baldwin and Rudyard Kipling.

MARGARET BURNE-JONES (1866–1954). Daughter of Georgiana and Edward Burne-Jones, *q.v.* She married J. W. Mackail, *q.v.*, Morris's first biographer.

PHILIP BURNE-JONES (1861–1926). Son of Georgiana and Edward Burne-Jones, *q.v.*

GEORGE CAMPFIELD. A glass painter. Foreman of the Morris Firm until 1898; according to Mackail he 'had come under Morris's notice as a pupil at the evening classes of the Working Men's College in Great Ormond St.'

AGLAIA CORONIO (1834–1906). Née Ionides; daughter of a wealthy Greek family, many of whom were patrons of the Pre-Raphaelites as well as of the Morris Firm. Although obviously not so dear to him as Georgiana Burne-Jones, *q.v.*, Aglaia was the recipient of many of Morris's more personal letters.

MARY AUGUSTA DE MORGAN (1850–1907). William De Morgan's sister, and friend of the Morris family, although she disapproved of Morris's Socialist views.

WILLIAM DE MORGAN (1839–1917). One of the best known ceramicists of the Arts and Crafts Movement; self-taught; produced tiles and lustre-ware. Worked for the Firm, and moved his workshops to Merton Abbey, to be near Morris, in 1882. Became well-known, during the last ten years of his life, as a novelist.

RICHARD WATSON DIXON (1833–1900). Was at school with Edward Burne-Jones, *q.v.*, and Cormell Price, *q.v.*; a member of the Oxford 'set' and contributor to the *Oxford and Cambridge Magazine*. He took Holy Orders and officiated at William and Jane Morris's wedding in Oxford. He later became Canon of Carlisle Cathedral.

FREDERICK STARTRIDGE ELLIS (1830–1901). Antiquarian book-seller;

Morris's friend, fellow-fisherman and publisher (publisher also of Swinburne, *q.v.*, and Rossetti, *q.v.*). Editor of several of the Kelmscott Press publications, including the *Chaucer*. He took over the joint tenancy of Kelmscott Manor after Rossetti left, and was one of Morris's executors.

WILLIAM HERBERT EVANS. An ex-army officer who contacted Morris when he heard about his trip to Iceland, and became the fourth member of the party, which included Eirikr Magnüsson, *q.v.*, and Charles Faulkner, *q.v.*

CHARLES JAMES FAULKNER (1834–1892). Mathematician and life-long friend of Morris, member of the Oxford 'set', and founder member of Morris, Marshall, Faulkner & Co. Was briefly business manager of the Firm, and accompanied Morris on the trips to Iceland. He supported all Morris's causes and founded the Oxford Branch of the Socialist League. Fellow of University College, Oxford.

KATE FAULKNER (d. 1898). Sister of Charles Faulkner, *q.v.*; designed and produced embroideries from the early days of the Firm. Also painted tiles and designed some wallpapers.

WILLIAM FULFORD (1832–1897). Undergraduate friend of Morris, and a member of the Oxford 'set'. He edited the *Oxford and Cambridge Magazine*.

FREDERICK BARLOW GUY. Morris's tutor before he went to Oxford; headmaster of Bradfield College.

GEORGE HOWARD (1843–1911). Ninth earl of Carlisle, Liberal MP, Morris's friend and patron of the Firm. Philip Webb, *q.v.*, built a church for the family at Brampton (near Naworth Castle, their Cumberland home), with stained glass by Burne-Jones, *q.v.*; Webb also designed the Howard's London residence at 1 Palace Green, which was decorated by Morris & Co.

ROSALIND HOWARD (1845–1921). Wife of George Howard, *q.v.* Friend of both Morris and Janey. She later became president of the Women's Liberal Federation and the National British Women's Temperance Association.

ARTHUR HUGHES (1832–1915). Pre-Raphaelite painter, also associated with the Oxford Union Mural scheme. Invited to be a founder member of the Firm, but declined for practical reasons.

FREDERICK LEACH. Decorator from Cambridge; Morris gave him several commissions, especially in the early years of the Firm.

GEORGIANA MACDONALD, see Georgiana Burne-Jones.

LOUISA MACDONALD, see Louisa Baldwin.

J. W. MACKAIL (1859–1945). First biographer of William Morris. Married Margaret Burne-Jones, *q.v.* Professor of Poetry at Oxford.

EIRIKR MAGNÜSSON (1833–1913). Taught Morris Icelandic and collaborated with him in translations; accompanied Morris on trip to Iceland.

PETER PAUL MARSHALL. 'By profession a surveyor and sanitary engineer at Tottenham' (Mackail). A friend of Ford Madox Brown, *q.v.*, and founder member of the Firm, for which he did little work in the early years. Left the Firm, with compensation, in 1875.

EMMA MORRIS. William Morris's eldest sister. Married Rev. Joseph Oldham, then curate of Walthamstow, in 1850.

JANE (JANEY) MORRIS (1839–1914). Daughter of Robert Burden, ostler, Oxford. Married William Morris in 1859. Produced embroidery for the Firm. Morris drew her and attempted to paint her portrait, but her features are now familiar from the many drawings and portraits made of her by her lover, Dante Gabriel Rossetti, *q.v.* Morris supported her, and, especially in the later years, there was obviously a close companionship between them.

JANE ALICE (JENNY) MORRIS (1861–1935). William Morris's elder daughter. Bright and intelligent as a young child, she was diagnosed as epileptic in 1876. Her illness, which was evidently serious, obviously distressed the family, and added to the strain of William and Janey's marriage.

MARY (MAY) MORRIS (1862–1938). William Morris's younger daughter. Studied at the South Kensington School of Design; produced embroidery for the Firm; in charge of the Firm's embroidery section from 1885. Shared her father's political commitment, and edited his *Collected Works* after his death (see Bibliography). Married Henry Halliday Sparling (then Secretary of the Socialist League) in 1890; the marriage broke down in 1894 ('The beautiful one banished him root and branch and resumed her maiden name' – George Bernard Shaw). Lived at Kelmscott Manor after her mother's death in 1914.

WILLIAM MORRIS Senior (1797–1847). William Morris's father; of Welsh descent, although the family had settled in Worcester in the latter part of the eighteenth century. Married Emma Shelton, *q.v.*, in 1826. He prospered as a partner in a firm of discount brokers, and his investment in the Devon Great Consols ensured the family's wealth for a number of years after his death.

ANTHONY JOHN MUNDELLA (1825–1897). MP for Sheffield (Radical); involved in Eastern Question movement.

CHARLES FAIRFAX MURRAY (1849–1919). Artist; friend of Rossetti and William Morris; did some work for the Firm, and contributed to the illustrations of *A Book of Verse*.

CHARLES ELIOT NORTON (1827–1908). American scholar who frequently visited England; friend of Ruskin, *q.v.*, and Morris.

VALENTINE (VAL) PRINSEP (1838–1904). Painter and friend of Rossetti, *q.v.*; contributed to the Oxford Union scheme.

CORMELL (CROM) PRICE (1836–1910). At school with Burne-Jones, *q.v.*; a member of the Oxford 'set', and a life-long friend of William Morris.

EDWARD PRINCE (1847–1923). Punch (type) cutter and craftsman printer. Cut Morris type for the Kelmscott Press. Gave punch-cutting classes at the Central School of Arts and Crafts, 1914–1918.

DANTE GABRIEL ROSSETTI (1828–1882). Painter and poet; founder member of the Pre-Raphaelite Brotherhood, 1848, and founder member of the Firm; contributed to stained glass and painted furniture. Married Elizabeth Siddal, *q.v.*, in 1859. Greatly admired by Morris when they first met. Jane Morris's lover from about 1867 to 1874.

WILLIAM ROSSETTI (1829–1919). Writer and civil servant; younger brother of Dante Gabriel, *q.v.*

JOHN RUSKIN (1819–1900). Influential writer on art and architecture, and social critic. He was a champion of the Pre-Raphaelites, and an inspiration to Morris and his colleagues, who first read his work while they were at Oxford. Ruskin's most influential book, as far as Morris was concerned, was *The Stones of Venice* (1851–1853); Morris was to reprint the chapter 'On the Nature of Gothic' at the Kelmscott Press.

ANDREAS SCHEU (1844–1927). Viennese furniture designer and Socialist exile; arrived London 1874. Met Morris when latter joined the Democratic Federation in 1883; founder, with Morris, of the Socialist League. Contributor to *The Commonweal*. Became a salesman for Jaeger in Edinburgh in 1885, and continued his political activities in Scotland.

GEORGE GILBERT SCOTT (1811–1878). Prolific architect, and enthusiastic restorer of ancient buildings. It was Scott's plans for Tewkesbury Abbey that prompted Morris to found the Society for the Protection of Ancient Buildings.

ELIZABETH (LIZZIE) SIDDAL (1834–1862). Model for the Pre-Raphaelites, especially Rossetti, *q.v.*, whom she married in 1859; committed suicide.

JOHN SPENCER STANHOPE (1829–1908). Painter, and friend of Rossetti, *q.v.* Contributed to the Oxford Union murals; also did some work for the Firm in the early years.

EDITH MARION STORY. The Marquess Edith Peruzzi. Lived in Rome where she got to know Robert Browning. Helped to supply Morris with vellum.

GEORGE EDMOND STREET (1824–1881). Architect dedicated to the Gothic Revival. Morris was briefly articled to him in 1856, when Street was architect to the Diocese of Oxford (Philip Webb, *q.v.*, was then Street's chief assistant). Designed the Law Courts, Strand, London, completed 1882.

ALGERNON CHARLES SWINBURNE (1837–1909). Poet and aesthete. Although their work was very different, Morris and he shared a mutual respect, and Morris, especially, valued his good opinion. Swinburne dedicated the 1898 volume of his poems to Morris and Burne-Jones.

GEORGE WARINGTON TAYLOR (1835–1870). Ex-Etonian and friend of Swinburne, *q.v.*, who introduced him to the Morris circle in the 1860s; appointed business manager of the Firm in 1865, and worked there until his early death (from tuberculosis). Urged order, economy and organization in a series of letters to Rossetti and Philip Webb (see page 40); contributed greatly to the economic survival of the Firm in the early years, and also reminded partners of their social responsibilities.

EMERY WALKER (1851–1933). Printer and typographer. Influential in the typographical revival in the latter part of the nineteenth century. Met Morris c. 1884, when he moved to a house in Hammersmith; supporter of the Society for the Protection of Ancient Buildings, as well as the Socialist League. Morris's personal enthusiasm for fine printing was revived when he attended a lecture given by Emery Walker to The Arts and Crafts Exhibition Society in 1888, and it was following this that he decided to set up the Kelmscott Press, with Walker's advice.

GEORGE WARDLE. Artist and draughtsman; manager of the Firm, 1870–1890; produced drawings (from medieval decorations in country churches) for the Firm. Introduced Morris to his brother-in-law Thomas Wardle, *q.v.*

THOMAS WARDLE (1831–1909). Owner of a dyeworks at Leek in Staffordshire, specialist in silk and cotton dyeing, and enthusiast in the revival of the use of non-chemical dyes. Collaborated with Morris from 1875, and, in spite of his frequent frustration with Morris's demands and exacting standards, remained a close friend.

PHILIP SPEAKMAN WEBB (1831–1915). Architect and life-long friend of Morris. Articled to Oxford architect G. E. Street, *q.v.*, where Morris and he met. Founder member of the Firm, and co-founder of the Society for the Protection of Ancient Buildings. Designed Red House, 1859, as well as several houses that were furnished by Morris & Co., including Standen in Sussex, Clouds in Wiltshire and Rounton Grange in Yorkshire.

LIST OF PLATES

Unless otherwise stated, all the work is by William Morris. Where dimensions are given the depth precedes the width.

LIST OF PLATES

56–7 EMBROIDERED PANELS, 1861
Three embroidered panels, designed for Red House, *c.* 1861;
made into a screen for the Earl of Carlisle, 1887.
Wool, silk and gold thread on serge with oak frame,
170.2 × 213.4 cm
Castle Howard Collection, York

58 CARTOON FOR ST. PAUL, *c.* 1862
Cartoon for glass, All Saints, Selsley, Gloucestershire.
Ink and watercolour, 68 × 49.5 cm (paper size)
William Morris Gallery, London
Photograph: Fine Art Photography

59 ST. PAUL, 1862
All Saints, Selsley, Gloucestershire
Stained glass, South Aisle window
Photograph: Sonia Halliday and Laura Lushington

60 STUDY FOR THE VIRGIN OF THE ANNUNCIATION, 1862
Black and grey washes over pencil, 66.8 × 49.5 cm (paper size)
All Saints, Selsley, Gloucestershire.
William Morris Gallery, London
Photograph: Ashmolean Museum

61 THE VIRGIN OF THE ANNUNCIATION, 1862
All Saints, Selsley, Gloucestershire
Stained glass, Chancel South Window
Photograph: D.J.R. Green

62 CARTOON FOR THE ANGEL OF THE ANNUNCIATION, 1862
Black and grey washes over pencil, 67 × 47 cm (paper size)
All Saints, Selsley, Gloucestershire
Ashmolean Museum, Oxford

63 THE ANGEL OF THE ANNUNCIATION, 1862
All Saints, Selsley, Gloucestershire
Stained glass, Chancel South Window
Photograph: D.J.R. Green

64 CARTOON FOR KING ARTHUR AND SIR LANCELOT, 1862
Sepia and watercolour (Arthur by William Morris; Lancelot by Ford
Madox Brown), for one of a series of windows illustrating *The Story
of Tristram*, originally for The Music Room, Harden Grange, Nr
Bingley, Yorkshire, 63.5 × 71.1 cm
Bradford Art Gallery and Museums

65 'IF I CAN' HANGING (detail), *c.* 1857
Embroidery wools on linen, designed and embroidered by William
Morris for Red Lion Square
Repeat size 72 × 29 cm, overall size 169 cm × 191 cm
The Trustees of the Kelmscott House Trust
Photograph: Peter Sanger

66 KING ARTHUR AND SIR LANCELOT
One of 13 stained-glass panels illustrating *The Story of Tristram*,
originally in The Music Room, Harden Grange, Nr Bingley,
Yorkshire
Bradford Art Gallery and Museums
Photograph: Richard Littlewood

67 QUEEN GUENEVERE AND ISOUDE LES BLANCHES MAINS
One of 13 stained glass panels illustrating *The Story of Tristram*
Bradford Art Gallery and Museums
Photograph: Richard Littlewood

68 Top PAINTED PANEL FOR ST. GEORGE'S CABINET, 1862
Panels painted by William Morris with scenes from the legend of
St. George
The cabinet itself was designed by Philip Webb
Victoria and Albert Museum, London

68 Bottom DESIGNS FOR PAINTED PANELS, ST. GEORGE'S
CABINET, 1861
Pen and wash, 44.4 × 15.5 cm (left), 43.8 × 35.3 cm (right)
Victoria and Albert Museum, London

69 DESIGN FOR PAINTED PANELS, ST. GEORGE'S CABINET, 1861
Pen and wash, 44.5 × 51 cm
Victoria and Albert Museum, London

70 DESIGN FOR TRELLIS WALLPAPER, 1862
Watercolour; with birds by Philip Webb; 66 × 58.4 cm (paper size)
William Morris Gallery, London
Photograph: Fine Art Photography

71 LOBBY, STANDEN
The lobby at Standen, with Trellis wallpaper (Standen, East
Grinstead, Sussex, was designed by Philip Webb in 1892)
Courtesy of The National Trust, Standen, Sussex
Photograph: Trevor Richards

72 DAISY WALLPAPER, 1862
The first wallpaper issued by Morris & Co., hand-printed for the
Firm by Jeffrey & Co.
Repeat size 35.5 × 26.6 cm
William Morris Gallery, London
Photograph: Fine Art Photography

73 DAISY HANGING, 1860
Embroidery, wool on serge, designed for Red House by William
Morris.
Embroidered by Janey Morris, Bessie Burden and friends; now in
Kelmscott Manor
The Trustees of the Kelmscott House Trust
Photograph: Trevor Richards

74 CARTOON FOR ARCHANGEL RAPHAEL *c.* 1862
From the studio of Ford Madox Brown, with face by William
Morris, for St. Michael and All Angels, Brighton
Sepia, 218 × 68.6 cm (paper size)
William Morris Gallery, London
Photograph: Fine Art Photography

75 ST. MICHAEL, ST. RAPHAEL, AND ST. MICHAEL AND THE
DRAGON, 1862
St. Michael and All Angels, Brighton (architect G.F. Bodley)
Stained glass West Windows, St. Michael by Ford Madox Brown;
Raphael by William Morris and St. Michael and the Dragon by P.P.
Marshall
Photograph: Duncan McNeill

76 FRUIT (OR POMEGRANATE) WALLPAPER, 1864
Repeat size 53.3 × 53.3 cm
William Morris Gallery, London
Photograph: Fine Art Photography

77 FRUIT WALLPAPER, 1864
Repeat size 53.3 × 53.3 cm
William Morris Gallery, London
Photograph: Fine Art Photography

78 EAST WINDOW, ALL SAINTS, MIDDLETON CHENEY,
NORTHAMPTONSHIRE, 1865
Stained glass by William Morris, E. Burne-Jones, P. Webb,
F. Madox Brown and S.J. Solomon
Photograph: Sonia Halliday Photographs

79 THE ANNUNCIATION, 1865
All Saints, Middleton Cheney, Northamptonshire
Stained glass, North Aisle
Photograph: Sonia Halliday Photographs

319

LIST OF PLATES

SELECT BIBLIOGRAPHY

May Morris published *The Collected Works of William Morris* in 24 volumes between 1910 and 1914; she also included additional material in *William Morris, Artist, Writer, Socialist,* 2 vols, London, 1934.

As well as popular editions of Morris's writings, the chief sources used are:

J. W. Mackail, *The Life of William Morris,* 2 vols, London, 1899.

Norman Kelvin, ed., *The Collected Letters of William Morris,* Vol. 1, 1848–1880, Princeton, 1984.

Philip Henderson, ed., *The Letters of William Morris to his Family and Friends,* London, 1950.

Ian Bradley, *William Morris and his World,* London, 1978.

Asa Briggs, ed., *William Morris: Selected Writings and Designs,* Harmondsworth, 1962.

Georgiana Burne-Jones, *Memorials of Edward Burne-Jones,* 2 vols, London, 1904.

Fiona Clark, *William Morris: Wallpaper and Chintzes,* London, 1973.

G. D. H. Cole, ed., *William Morris: Selected Writings,* London, 1934.

Oliver Fairclough and Emeline Leary, *Textiles by William Morris and Morris & Co., 1861–1940,* London, 1981.

Peter Faulkner, *Against the Age. An Introduction to William Morris,* London, 1980.

Peter Faulkner, *William Morris and W. B. Yeats,* Dublin and Oxford, 1962.

Peter Faulkner, ed., *William Morris: The Criticial Heritage,* London 1973.

Delbert R. Gardner, *An ''Idle Singer'' and his Audience,* The Hague and Paris, 1975.

Amanda Hodgson, *The Romances of William Morris,* Cambridge, 1987.

Eugene D. Lemire, ed., *The Unpublished Lectures of William Morris,* Michigan, 1969.

Jack Lindsay, *William Morris: His Life and Work,* London, 1975.

Roderick Marshall, *William Morris and his Earthly Paradise,* Tisbury, 1979.

Paul Meier, *William Morris: The Marxist Dreamer,* 2 vols, London, 1978.

Barbara Morris, *Inspiration for Design: The Influence of the Victoria and Albert Museum,* London, 1986.

A. L. Morton, ed., *The Political Writings of William Morris,* London, 1979.

Gillian Naylor, *The Arts and Crafts Movement,* London, 1971.

Linda Parry, *William Morris Textiles,* London, 1983.

Charles Sewter, *The Stained Glass of William Morris,* 2 vols, New Haven, 1974.

Peter Stansky, *Redesigning the World,* Princeton, 1985.

E. P. Thompson, *William Morris: Romantic to Revolutionary,* London, 1955.

Paul Thompson, *The Work of William Morris,* London, 1967.

Aymer Vallance, *William Morris: His Art, his Writings and his Public Life,* London, 1897.

Ray Watkinson, *William Morris as Designer,* London, 1967.

Catalogues

Morris and Company, Fine Art Society, 1979.

Morris and Company in Cambridge, Fitzwilliam Museum, Cambridge, 1980.

William Morris and Kelmscott, Farnham School of Art, 1981.

William Morris and the Middle Ages, Whitworth Art Gallery, Manchester, 1984.

William Morris Today, Institute of Contemporary Arts, London, 1984.

Textiles by William Morris and Morris & Co. 1861–1940, Birmingham Art Gallery, 1981.

The Typographical Adventure of William Morris, William Morris Society, 1958.

List of houses which include decorations by William Morris:

Red House	The Oxford Union
Bexleyheath	Oxford University
Kent	Oxford
Kelmscott Manor	Queens' College
Kelmscott	Cambridge
Oxfordshire	
	The William Morris Room
Standen	The Victoria and Albert Museum
East Grinstead	Cromwell Road
West Sussex	South Kensington
	London SW7
Wightwick Manor	
Wolverhampton	The William Morris Gallery
West Midlands	Lloyd Park
	Forest Road
Linley Sambourne House	Walthamstow
Kensington	London E17
London SW7	
Jesus College	
Cambridge	